FOR THE

o be returned on or
last date below.

o May

FAITH FOR THE FUTURE

*Essays on the Church in Education
to mark 175 years of the National Society*

Editor-in-chief
GRAHAM LEONARD
Bishop of London

Editor
JOANNA YATES

National Society
Church House Publishing

W 32427 £4.95' 1·87

ISBN 0 7151 4759 5

Jointly published by
The National Society
and Church House Publishing
Church House, Great Smith Street, London SW1P 3NZ

Designed by Bill Bruce at THE CREATIVE HOUSE and typeset in 11/12pt Palatino

Printed in England by The Print Business

Preface

When this book was in preparation the Editors received valuable advice from members of the National Society Standing Committee and others. Special thanks are due to Mr Peter Gedge of St Martin's College of Higher Education, Lancaster, for his help in planning the contents, to Canon Patrick Appleford and to the Revd Francis Stephens. Thanks are also extended to Mrs Pamela Egan, Publications Officer of the General Synod Board of Education, for her help, and to Mr Robin Brookes and his staff for their contribution towards this first joint venture of the National Society and Church House Publishing.

The Editors are grateful to members of the National Society's staff who have helped in a number of ways. Mr Colin Alves, General Secretary, read the book in typescript and made many useful suggestions. Mr Geoffrey Duncan, the Revd Ian Pearson and Mr Alan Brown gave valuable assistance, and the manuscript was typed with exemplary care by Mrs Julia Hall.

Editors

Graham Leonard, Editor-in-Chief, has been Bishop of London since 1981. He is Chairman of the National Society and of the Church of England General Synod Board of Education. From 1958 to 1962 he was General Secretary of the National Society and Secretary of the Church of England Schools Council. He was consecrated Bishop of Willesden in 1964 and translated to Truro in 1973. He was formerly Chairman of the General Synod Board for Social Responsibility, and is now Chairman of the BBC and IBA Central Religious Advisory Committee. Among his many publications are *God Alive: Priorities in Pastoral Theology* (1982), *Firmly I Believe and Truly* (1985) and contributions to *Is Christianity Credible?* (1981) and *The Cross and the Bomb* (1983).

Joanna Yates, Editor, read Literae Humaniores at Oxford and trained as a teacher at King's College, London. She taught classics in London schools and in the field of adult education for thirteen years, until in 1985 she became Promotions and Publications Secretary of the National Society and Editor of the magazine *Crosscurrent.*

Contributors

Gordon Huelin is a former Lecturer in Theology in the University of London and Professor of Divinity at Gresham College. He has been a Fellow of King's College, London since 1978 and is also a Fellow of the Society of Antiquaries. He is Associate Professor of Theology in the University of Notre Dame, Indiana (London Program) and Archivist and Librarian of SPCK. He has published many theological and historical books and articles, including *King's College, London 1928-1978*.

Robert Holtby, Dean of Chichester since 1977, was the first joint General Secretary of the National Society (1967-1977) and the Church of England General Synod Board of Education (1974-1977). Previously he was Director of Education in the Diocese of Carlisle. His publications include *Daniel Waterland, A Study in 18th Century Orthodoxy* (1966) and *Eric Graham, 1888-1964* (1967). He has just completed a biography of Robert Stopford, to be published shortly.

Stewart Sutherland, Principal of King's College, London, was Professor of the History and Philosophy of Religion from 1977 to 1985. He was formerly a Lecturer at the University College of North Wales and at Stirling University. He is President of the Society for the Study of Theology and has been Editor of *Religious Studies* since 1984. His many philosophical and theological publications include *The Philosophical Frontiers of Christian Theology* (1983), *God, Jesus and Belief* (1984) and *Faith and Ambiguity* (1984).

Basil Mitchell was Nolloth Professor of the Philosophy of the Christian Religion in the University of Oxford from 1968 to 1984, and is an Emeritus Fellow of Oriel College. He has been a member of Church of England working parties on ethical questions, and the Doctrine Commission. He was also a member of the Commission on Religious Education in Schools which produced *The Fourth R.* He has published many philosophical and theological articles and books, including *Law, Morality and Religion in a Secular Society* (1967), *The Justification of Religious Belief* (1973) and *Morality: Religious and Secular* (1980).

David Hargreaves has been Chief Inspector of the Inner London Education Authority since 1984. He was previously a Lecturer and Reader in Education at the University of Manchester and a Fellow of Jesus College, Oxford. He is the author of several publications on the secondary school, including *Social Relations in a Secondary School* (1967) and *The Challenge for the Comprehensive School* (1982).

John Gwinnell taught geography and careers for fourteen years at schools in Hertfordshire, before becoming Vice-Principal of Stockton-on-Tees Grammar School. He was Headteacher of St Edward's Church of England Secondary School, Romford until 1985, and is now Principal of Wilberforce Sixth Form College, Hull. He is a member of the Advisory Council for the Church's Ministry Vocations Committee.

Geoffrey Duncan is Deputy Secretary and Schools Officer of the National Society, and Schools Secretary of the General Synod Board of Education. He served in the Royal Army Educational Corps and was a schoolteacher and technical college lecturer, before becoming a local education authority adviser on further education and then deputy area education officer; he has contributed articles on education to several journals. He is a Reader in the Diocese of Chichester.

David Barton is Headteacher of Soho Parish School. He was ordained priest in 1966 and served in a country group of parishes, before training as a teacher at Goldsmiths' College, London. He has worked in London schools for the past fifteen years and is a non-stipendiary minister in the Diocese of London, attached to St James' Church, Piccadilly.

Clive Jones-Davies, Principal of Trinity College of Higher Education, Carmarthen since 1980, was formerly Deputy Secretary and Schools Officer of the National Society and Schools Secretary of the General Synod Board of Education. He previously taught in secondary schools, and then served as a senior educational psychologist, adviser in special education and assistant education officer successively in three local education authorities: Cambridgeshire, Gloucestershire and Cleveland. His publications include, as editor, *The Slow Learner in the Secondary School* (1975) and *The Disruptive Pupil in the Secondary School* (1976).

Colin Alves has been General Secretary of the National Society and of the General Synod Board of Education since 1984. He was formerly a lecturer at King Alfred's College of Higher Education, Winchester, Head of Religious Studies at Brighton College of Education, Director of the RE Centre at St Gabriel's College and Colleges Officer of the General Synod Board of Education. He was a member of the Durham Commission on RE and Chairman of the Schools Council RE Committee, and was Secretary of the Association of Voluntary Colleges from 1978 to 1984. Among his publications are *Religion and the Secondary School* (1968) and *The Christian in Education* (1972).

Contents

Foreword

During the last few years education has developed a much higher profile, so much so that it was suggested recently that it could be a major factor at the next General Election. On the part of the general public and particularly of parents, two concerns have been predominant. The first is expressed in the widespread desire for an improvement in the standard of education. The second represents an aversion to the use of the education system as a means of forwarding the aims of a particular political ideology, by, for example, restrictions on text books used or the appointment of governors on political grounds. The situation is confused by the fact that the present government, while favouring greater central control over education in certain respects, is also seeking in the Education Bill now before the House of Commons to strengthen the powers of governors, ensure that they are more representative of the local community which is served by a school, and limit the powers of Local Education Authorities.

When I was General Secretary of the National Society some thirty years ago I was asked to address those from other countries on our education system. I used to point out that our maintained schools were not State schools. They were county or voluntary schools, the State, as such, having very limited powers in their conduct or curriculum. The situation has now changed and successive governments have taken increasing powers. In a recent television interview, the Secretary of State for Education and Science used the term State schools without apology, though it is still, strictly speaking, incorrect.

The position is further complicated by the problems created for education by our multicultural and multifaith society, particularly in the centres of our cities, and those created in the rural areas by depopulation with its effect on the size and viability of village schools. To these must be added the pressures for education, particularly in the universities and polytechnics, to be more directly related to the industrial and technological needs of this country, pressures which come at a time when intellectual thought is moving in the direction of recognising the need for the sciences and the arts to complement each other rather than being regarded as alternatives.

It is against this background that the National Society has to assess its future role as it celebrates the 175th Anniversary of its foundation in 1811. In 1953, it set out a five-point policy in anticipation of the establishment in 1958 of the official Board of Education, which assumed certain functions and responsibilities hitherto exercised by the Society. Two of the five points recognised its continued responsibility to initiate and develop thought on the subject of religious education, and in the years which followed it sought to do so, as, for example, in its sponsorship of the Durham Commission which produced the Report, *The Fourth R* in 1970.

The need is now evident for the development of an even deeper and more far-reaching philosophy of Christian education, for that is what the present situation demands. Such is the case not merely when matters of major policy are being discussed. Some aspects of the continuing work of the Society, such as the provision of advice, educational and legal, to Diocesan Directors of Education and individual governing bodies, frequently raise deeper questions which cannot be answered simply on the basis of law, expediency or efficiency.

One of the great merits of this collection of essays is that both in terms of philosophy and theology and of the concrete needs of schools and colleges it reveals this urgent need to respond to the present situation by sustained thought about the purpose and nature of education and of Christian education in particular.

The first two essays, by Dr Gordon Huelin and the Dean of Chichester, root the book firmly in the history of the Society, recalling in splendidly succinct but attractive ways how it has developed and adapted itself to changing situations over the years, and has always sought to do so in partnership with government, whether local or central.

Professor Sutherland and Professor Mitchell in their essays have clear implications for the future policy of the Society. The conclusion which seems to me to flow from what they write is that it has a prime duty, now and in the immediate future, to take steps to encourage the development of a Christian and coherent basis for education which takes account of recent changes both in intellectual thought and in the pattern of society. To some extent, the process was initiated in the Society's recent publication, *A Future in Partnership,* which received and deserved an encouraging response. Nevertheless, it was generally recognised in the debate on it that more work was needed on the theological basis of education and on the relationship between theology and education. The present debates on history and theology and the state of Biblical scholarship do not make this an easy task, but educationalists can and must contribute to the thinking of theologians and Biblical scholars, just as they can and must contribute to ours. Educationalists must not wait until the Biblical scholars arrive at what are judged to be assured results.

Professor Sutherland makes a justified, telling and necessary point when he says that 'Whatever the cause, theologians within the Church and ecclesiastical leaders have failed miserably to educate most believers theologically much beyond an elementary Sunday school level.' Yet it is these who, so inadequately equipped, have to take an increasingly important role as governors of our Church schools; and those who come to train as teachers of religious education are often less well-equipped to begin their training than those who specialise in other subjects. Professor Sutherland draws attention to the pressures of relativism, materialism and behaviourism which undermine human freedom and responsibility. He says that 'to its considerable credit, unlike the physical sciences, the biological sciences, the psychological and social sciences (economics, history and sociology) and the "educational sciences", monotheistic theology has never even flirted with, let alone espoused, any form of materialism or behaviourism'. But one must ask how many teachers of religious education have appreciated that this is so. Professor Mitchell refers to the unhappy distinction between 'values' and facts, and emphasises the need for thinking and feeling to be related not only in religious education but in every aspect of learning. His essay is a powerful plea for an understanding of religious education which embraces the whole person and all human activities.

The same points are reflected in Dr Hargreaves' comments on the disposition of some RE teachers to confine themselves to a narrow view of the subject which 'refuses to take any risks and defensively maintains itself as a completely separate and distinctive subject'. He draws attention to the urgent need for a review of 'the education and teacher training of the RE specialist, including late in-service training' which will enable the teacher to relate it to the curriculum as a whole. A like need is evident in Mr Gwinnell's essay on Worship. Only if such a coherent Christian view of education, based on the Biblical understanding of man, responsible and free, yet a member of the community, part of the created world yet made to live with God, is the basis of the life of our Church schools will Mr Duncan's insistence on the need for them to be distinctive be met. It must also be the basis of our approach to the multiracial nature of our society, if it is to be both truly Christian and truly human.

To visit Fr Barton's school in Soho, which he describes vividly in his essay, is a remarkable experience. Quite evidently a Christian school, it has become a place of harmony and co-operation, by emphasis on the family and on the religious nature of man. The need for such a coherent philosophy is especially great in Higher Education, as Mr Jones-Davies makes clear.

The Society is greatly indebted to those who have contributed these essays, giving generously of their wisdom, skill and experience. Together they present an unmistakeable need which must be met both by the Society and by all who are concerned with Christian education. I hope and pray that our thanksgiving at this time may be expressed by a disciplined and whole-hearted response to the call of the authors and that thereby we may be enabled both to respond to the present situation in education and lay solid foundations for the future.

+ Graham London

Bishop of London

1

Innovation:
The National Society 1811-1934

Gordon Huelin

When William Francis Cowper-Temple declared in the House of Commons in 1837 that popular education in England 'originated with no statesman' but 'sprang from the action of the Church and the philanthropy of individuals',[1] he was not being complimentary; he was speaking the truth. High on the roll of honour in what was a battlefield must stand the names of those who launched and carried on the work of 'the National Society for promoting the Education of the Poor in the Principles of the Established Church throughout England and Wales'.

A battlefield? Indeed: though when in the summer of 1811 the Society's three founders Joshua Watson, Henry Norris and John Bowles,[2] all old-fashioned High Churchmen, met to discuss what they could do to help the masses of poor people who, despite the existence of charity schools and Sunday schools, had no opportunity of receiving even the most elementary education, they can have had little idea of the magnitude of the struggle ahead. Forty-five years later, in a letter to the Society's Secretary, the Bishop of London, Charles James Blomfield, would describe the opposing forces as 'the multiplied attempts of philosophical or political theorists to introduce their systems of merely secular teaching, or of a religious teaching so restricted and so generalised as to be comparatively inoperative'.[3] Yet, initially, there was much encouragement for the National Society. First, it had the goodwill of the Archbishop of Canterbury, Charles

Manners-Sutton, who not only took the chair at its inaugural gathering on October 16, 1811, but also presided whenever he could over the fortnightly meetings. Second, there were the voluntary donations which poured in from well-wishers within a short time of its foundation.

The contribution made by the parochial clergy in supporting the Society's work, and in furthering its aim of planting a school in every parish in the land where instruction should be given both in religion and in the three Rs, is incalculable. In fact, a survey made by the Society during the 1840s into the state and progress of its schools throughout England and Wales revealed that the clergy were not only largely responsible for taking the initiative in founding schools, but also for maintaining them. Such entries as 'the expense mainly falls upon the vicar', and 'the incumbent has built three cottages, which he has converted into schoolrooms and dwelling for the mistress at his own expense, with the exception of seven guineas from Mr and Mrs Twopenny,[4] were common. Again, one of the H.M. Inspectors reported that from his own examination of nearly two hundred examples he was convinced that, with few exceptions, the clergy took a deep interest in their schools. There were instances where the parish priest, after giving morning instruction in the day school, returned to teach at night; others where when the master was away he took the absentee's place; and still others where in order to make up the master's salary or pay for repairs he willingly dipped into his own pocket.[5]

The political and theological climate of the nineteenth century was such that the opposing forces which the National Society had to face numbered not only the employers, such as farmers who were prejudiced against their workers' being given what they regarded as unnecessary education, but also those fellow-Christians who at that time were still referred to as 'Dissenters'. Already, when the Society was launched in 1811, there was in existence an organised body gathered around Joseph Lancaster, a Quaker, which in 1814 became 'The British and Foreign Schools Society' whose aim was to promote 'the Education of the Labouring and Manufacturing Classes of Society of every Religious Persuasion'. Although the method of teaching known as the 'monitorial system', whereby children were taught by other children in the class, was common to both Societies, there was a fundamental difference in the content of the religious instruction. The National Society, as a Church of England institution, maintained that in the 'National' schools such instruction should include the Prayer Book and Catechism as well as the Bible. The British and Foreign Schools Society, supported by the Dissenters as well as by some liberal Anglicans, insisted that religious instruction in the 'British' schools should be confined to Scripture and 'general Christian principles'. It was this difference which in days to come became the cause of intense bitterness between Christians in opposite camps, and which impeded what ought to have been a common purpose. It is an unhappy story which cannot be glossed over: but first there are matters of a more fruitful nature to consider.

During its early years, the National Society relied for teaching purposes on the 'monitorial system', which had the great merit of being cheap. There were, however serious disadvantages, not least that it was largely a case of learning by rote, and if a visiting examiner should happen to reverse the order of questions to which the children had grown accustomed, the result could be chaotic! So when in 1833 the State made its first grant towards school buildings – the greater part of which went to the National Society – a proposal was put forward to set up Teachers' Training Colleges. The first of such colleges was opened in 1841 – that of St. Mark, Chelsea, for men. It was followed by Whitelands College – also then in Chelsea – for women, the rules of which, as laid down by the Society's committee with a view to 'promoting simplicity of dress among the mistresses in training', make amusing reading today.[6] The third of these colleges was at Battersea, where training was concentrated on the mining and agricultural areas of the country.

In order to help teachers and students in the training colleges, the Society in 1845 opened its own 'Depository'. Bound up with its Annual Report will frequently be found a catalogue of publications which, in addition to Scriptural material, included books on reading, spelling and grammar, arithmetic and mathematics, music, geography with maps and atlases, and 'new prize books for the young'.[7] A visitor to the National Society's bookshop in the 1930s would have had to be content with a more limited range!

One has to bear in mind the fact that the Society's mission was not simply to England but, as its title then proclaimed, to Wales also. So that this obligation should be fulfilled a fourth college was founded at Carmarthen with the intention of training Welsh students for Welsh 'National' schools. In Wales, however, the development of elementary education faced special problems. These were due to poverty, and to the fact that a much greater proportion of the population was Nonconformist, particularly in South Wales where parents were reluctant to send their children to Church schools. The Annual Reports, which contain details of progress made in Wales, often sound a pessimistic note: as when one of the clergy responsible for the area commented that the Society had no representatives in the poorer parts of Wales, and feared it would 'be very difficult for anyone undertaking such an office to gain support in return for his labours'.[8] This brings us back to the problems referred to earlier.

While Churchmen could feel proud that it was the Church and not the State which had taken the initiative as regards popular education in England, they became increasingly aware as time went on that no amount of generosity and self-sacrifice on their part would be sufficient to maintain the growing number of schools up and down the country. In 1833 there came the first government grant. Six years later a special Committee of Council on Education was set up: and this not only favoured non-sectarian teaching, but also insisted on the right to inspect all schools participating in the Parliamentary grant. There followed what has been called 'the first quarrel with Caesar'.[9]

Nothing illustrates more clearly the intensity of feeling on the part of Churchmen faced with the threat of unsectarian education in schools than *The Times'* account of a meeting arranged by members and friends of the National Society at Willis's Rooms, King Street, St James's, on May 28, 1839: 'The chair was announced to be taken by his Grace the Archbishop of Canterbury at 2 o'clock, but long ere that hour, or indeed 1 o'clock, had arrived the street was literally crammed with carriages, and crowds of fashionably dressed ladies, of nobility as well as commoners, formed an almost impenetrable phalanx on the footway leading from St James's Square and St James's Street. Among the fairer sex, too, were to be seen many of the right rev. prelates and numerous members of both branches of the legislative supported by others of high consideration in the country. Within a very few minutes of the doors having been opened the large room was filled in every corner'.[10]

As a protest against the Committee of Council on Education's insistence on State inspection of schools, Joshua Watson, the leading spirit in founding the National Society, resigned from the post of its treasurer after more than thirty years.[11] An even more militant opponent of State inspection, G.A. Denison, wrote to the Clerical Inspector of Schools: 'My dear Bellairs, I love you very much; but if you ever come here again to inspect, I lock the door of the school and tell the boys to put you in the pond'.[12]

A further difficulty arose from the stand adopted by Nonconformist parents against their children at Church schools' being forced to attend lessons on the Prayer Book and Catechism. A 'conscience clause', giving them leave of absence, would have solved the problem and there were some Anglicans who recognised the reasonableness of such a course of action. But religious toleration in the Victorian age still had to face an uphill road. The National Society remained adamant in its attitude of 'no compromise', an attitude particularly resented in areas where there was a single Church school. 'Perhaps nothing in the educational controversies of the nineteenth century did more to influence denominational bitterness than the Anglican refusal to concede rights of conscience, for it bred deep resentment and distress which were to rankle in dissenting hearts for many years to come'.[13]

Regrettable as this was, it should not be allowed to detract from the National Society's achievements, of which some assessment was made in the Annual Report published as it approached its seventieth birthday. Looking back, this recalled how for some years after its establishment its work had been of a missionary character: with many deep-seated prejudices against the diffusion of education to be overcome; its own principles to be defined; teachers to be provided and books prepared. Then had come the tardy assistance of the State, with the funds made available enabling the Society to set up new schools. The year 1839 had seen the coming into existence of the Committee of Council on Education, with the

State now working in concert with the Church in the advancement of religious as well as of secular teaching. Finally, there was the passing of the Education Act of 1870 and the consequent necessity for the Church through the agency of the National Society to sustain the work which the State then abandoned. Taking stock, the Society pointed out that while it had endeavoured to adapt its organisation and methods to the changing times and needs, the principle embodied in its Charter, namely that all true education must be based upon religion, remained unaltered.[14] Surely, however, the finest testimony to what the Society had by then achieved lay not in the pages of printed Reports, but in the existence of well over 6,700 Church schools, providing education for something like a million and a half children.

Differences over education between Anglicans and Free Churchmen continued to arouse strife during the early years of the twentieth century. There were, it must be said, faults on both sides. Robert Stopford, a distinguished educationalist and a former Bishop of London, has drawn attention to the suffering caused, on the one hand to the children since 'the religious instruction which should have given unity and purpose to all the teaching was divorced from the life of the Church', and, on the other hand to the Churches themselves, since through mutual hostility they lost the opportunity of winning back the great mass of the working classes.[15]

In 1911 the National Society celebrated its centenary. At a meeting held on October 16, exactly one hundred years to the day of its foundation, the Archbishop of Canterbury, Randall Davidson, emphasized its unique contribution to religious education. A noticeable feature of these celebrations was the desire to do justice to the work of the Nonconformists in this field.[16]

As the century advanced, it became increasingly apparent that both the Constitution of the Society and its name were out of keeping with modern ideas. Accordingly, when in April 1934 King George V granted a Supplemental Charter, it was agreed that the original title should be changed to 'The National Society for Promoting Religious Education in accordance with the Principles of the Church of England', or, for short, 'The National Society'. The disestablishment of the Anglican Church in Wales in 1920 had led to fears that the Society might in future concentrate its efforts only on Church schools in England. Hence the Charter contained an important provision that it should 'as hitherto operate in England and Wales and not in England alone'.

That year's Annual Report drew attention to the parallels between the early years of the Society's existence and the troubled period of the 1930s. Fair enough: but there was one very significant difference, in that full credit was now given not only to the founders of the National Society but also to those of the British and Foreign Schools Society and of the other denominational school organisations. To quote the Report: 'It would probably be impossible to overrate the effective contribution which *their* (my italics) magnificent efforts for religious education made'.[17] Such a recognition meant the ending of suspicion and rivalry and the birth of a new spirit of understanding and co-operation.

1 C.K. Francis Brown, *The Church's Part in Education* 1833-1941, National Society and SPCK, 1942, title page.
2 E. Churton (editor), *A Memoir of Joshua Watson*, J.H. and James Parker, 1864, vol. 1, 103.
3 *ibid*, page 122.
4 C.K. Francis Brown, *op cit*, pages 11-12.
5 *ibid*.
6 H.J. Burgess, *Enterprise in Education*, NS and SPCK, 1958, page 116.
7 For example, *NS Annual Report* 1899.
8 The Revd C.F. Rogers in *NS Annual Report* 1878.
9 H.J. Burgess, *op cit.*, Chapter 7.
10 *The Times*, 29th May 1839, page 5.
11 A.B. Webster, *Joshua Watson*, SPCK 1954, page 40.
12 Owen Chadwick, *The Victorian Church*, A & C Black, 1970, Part 1, page 344.
13 M. Cruickshank, *Church and State in English Education*, Macmillan, 1963, page 10; quoted with approval by Robert Stopford.
14 *NS Annual Report* 1880.
15 Robert Stopford, *Christian Education and Unity*, in *Religious Education 1944-1984*, edited by A.G. Wedderspoon, Allen and Unwin, 1966.
16 *NS Annual Report* 1912.
17 *NS Annual Report* 1934.

2
Duality:
The National Society 1934-1986
Robert Holtby

'We must say what it is about the dual system that we believe in: and why the thing we believe in can be secured by the dual system and in no other way'.[1] This was Archbishop William Temple's challenge to the Society in his Presidential Address on 3 June, 1942, and he gave as one of the values of the dual system its duality. The address might have been called 'a future in partnership', and it was remarkably prophetic in its estimate of educational development: growing professionalism among teachers, increased expertise in educational administration, the reorganisation of schools, co-operation with other Christian bodies in education, and the teasing question of the right relationship between Church and school – here was an agenda for the years ahead. Three years earlier Temple had been chairman of a committee which issued an interim report on the dual system, and this was followed by a survey of Church schools and the Society's memorandum of September, 1942, accepted by the Church Assembly in February, 1943. The interim report, *inter alia,* had urged a coherent system of diocesan educational administration, and the Society, from 1934 onwards, had endeavoured to reform its own committee structures to match the areas of its educational work. Temple was quite clear that there should be no surrender of Church schools, and rejected the possibility of the wholesale transfer of Church schools in 'single school areas'. Yet he advocated the *adaptation of tradition* to meet the needs of the day – to enable co-operation with the Free Churches, and to foster partnership with public authorities. In 1941 the Archbishops of Canterbury, York and Wales had published their 'five points', which set out a policy for religious education: religious instruction was to be given in all schools, subject to a conscience clause; the school day to begin with a collective act of worship; religious instruction not to be confined to any particular period of the day; agreed syllabus instruction to be open to inspection; and religious knowledge to be a recognised subject for the teachers' certificate. The way was being prepared for the negotiations leading to the Education Act, and discussions with Free Churchmen were of crucial importance in forging relationships necessary for securing agreement on the religious clauses. In 1940 Free Church representatives had joined the three Archbishops in a deputation to meet the President of the Board of Education. Temple's reputation, not least in ecumenical endeavour, was a factor of immense importance.

Already the partnership between Church and State had been widened in scope. The supplemental Charter of 1934 enlarged the Society's field of work, and consequently it was recognised as the Church's Central Council for Religious Education (recognised as such also by the Governing Body of the Church in Wales). This ensued from the Hadow Report of 1929. The Education Act of 1936 raised the school leaving age, and made provision for Church senior schools ('Special Agreement' schools) with grants of 50 per cent to 75 per cent, thus involving the Society in the duty of providing advice and assistance to dioceses on legal, financial and other matters arising from the new opportunity within the maintained system, and the Church Assembly in 1939 voted £2,500 to the Society for 'new Charter' work. But there were wider fields of activity: the Sunday School Institute and the Church Tutorial Classes Association were amalgamated with the Society, and in 1939 the Publications Committee was established. Further, the appearance in 1938 of Phyllis Dent's *New Approach*[2] was indicative of concern with content and method in religious education, not simply with institutions. Here was a passionate concern for children, anticipating later thinking about the priority of the person rather than that of the syllabus, yet founded on unambiguous Christian conviction.

The war inevitably set back some of the business. The working headquarters moved to Chichester, some of it occupying the Deanery dining room. But the promise in the 1942 speech began to be realised once thoughts turned to post-war reconstruction. 1943 saw the first Diocesan Education Committees Measure (revised in 1955), laying the foundations for the Church's major tasks in the years ahead, and in the same year the White Paper on Educational Reconstruction was issued by the Coalition Government. Temple discussed the religious clauses with R.A. Butler, and Henry Brooke, MP for West Lewisham, was the Church's 'watchdog' in the House of Commons. The General Secretary, Canon E.F. Hall,[3] did much of the spade-work on the religious clauses, and to no officer in its whole history is the Society more indebted than to him.

The system which emerged in the 1933 Act is still the basis of educational provision in England and Wales, and George Bell, Bishop of Chichester, failed in the Church Assembly to gain the support for a modified version of the Scottish system for voluntary schools.

The Society now had to advise on the new arrangements for voluntary schools, Aided and Controlled, and on the implementation of the Development Plans which each local education authority had to make in accordance with the provisions of the Act. The fulfilment of this grand design in education – the remodelling of old buildings, the redisposition of schools, and the erection of new premises – was accomplished over decades, and it was helped on the financial side by the creation of what were known as 'Barchester' schemes, contributory schemes on a diocesan basis, enabling school redevelopment to be funded co-operatively. Successive officers of the Society were deeply indebted to Mr J.L.B. Todhunter of the Legal Branch of the (then) Ministry of Education, who displayed zeal for Church schools and their financing, with theological and genealogical insights. The Society therefore became deeply engaged in the working out of the Principal Act and in the consequences of subsequent legislation, notably the Acts of 1946, of 1959 (which raised the grant to 75 per cent), of 1967 (to 80 per cent) and 1974 (to 85 per cent). In addition there were the further developments in school reorganisation, notably a provision in the 1959 Act allowing 'matching' secondary schools, and the comprehensive reorganisation stemming from the seminal circular 10/65. The Society had to give its attention to the possibility, canvassed in some political quarters, of the consolidation of legislation and even of a new Act. In 1970 the then Labour Government hoped to pass an Act to mark the centenary of that of 1870, and the Society, together with the Board of Education of the Church Assembly (General Synod), prepared evidence. In the event, however, the Conservative Government dropped the scheme, the new Secretary of State, Mrs Margaret Thatcher, considering a new bill unnecessary. The Society had the pleasure of greeting her at its great service in St Paul's Cathedral to mark the centenary of the 1870 Act, when the preacher was the Headmaster of a comprehensive school named after Robert Stopford, Bishop of London and former General Secretary.

We have seen that the Society was the Central Council for Religious Education both in England and Wales, but increasingly this situation proved to be anomalous. Its function as a Central Council could not be incorporated in its Charter, and its responsibilities covered Wales, over which the Church Assembly had no jurisdiction. Furthermore, the Church of England Youth Council had been established in 1935 and was made an official Council of the Assembly in 1942, and, like the Council of Church Training Colleges, reconstituted in 1944, was independent of the Society. In 1945 therefore a Commission under Lord Selborne was appointed to consider the whole position. The Commission reported in 1946 to the Archbishop of Canterbury:

> In vesting the National Society with the functions of the Central Council of the Church of England for Religious Education, while refusing to endorse the complementary radical changes in its constitution which the 1929 Commission had postulated, the Church Assembly has in fact imposed functions on a machine designed for a different purpose.[4]

The Commission concluded that the Society could not remain a voluntary society and at the same time be an official council of the Church. Thus in 1947 the Church Assembly set up a Council for Education, directly responsible to it, with five departmental Councils. The new Council never worked satisfactorily, and in 1958 the Board of Education replaced it. Even so, the National Society in many ways continued to be regarded by the dioceses as the Church's principal educational agency, not least because its General Secretary under the new arrangements was also Secretary of the Schools Council and chairman of regular meetings of diocesan Directors of Education. The situation imposed upon the two General Secretaries (of the National Society and the Board) difficulties concerning their respective spheres of operation.

It was perhaps significant of the role of the Society that in 1970 the Secretary of State addressed his first enquiry about evidence on a new Education Act to the National Society rather than to the (official) Board. In due course both the Society and the Board accepted a document, *Going Forward Together,* (signed on 13th December, 1972 by the two General Secretaries), by which it was agreed that neither body would do separately what could be done together, that Deputy Secretaries would be shared, and that in due course one officer would be General Secretary of both bodies. This last intention was fulfilled in 1974, and it was greatly helped by the fact that the Society had left the premises in Great Peter Street and moved to rooms in Church House adjacent to the Board of Education. Meanwhile, in 1972 a further Supplemental Charter was granted, which enabled the Society to extend its activities anywhere in the world, to release it from any obligation to divide the application of its assets, and to provide a more efficient committee structure.

In the sixties the Society had to consider seriously a number of reports on primary, secondary and further education, including in 1968 the Gittins Report on Primary Education in Wales.

It organised conferences on schools administration, and it continued to convene informal meetings of diocesan directors of education. From 1969 the Library and Archives sections (one of the most important collections in the Kingdom), were reorganised, and the many thousands of school files continued to be of use for schools throughout England and Wales. Day by day advice was, and is, given to dioceses, parishes, and individual schools, not least on legal questions, and on the last the readily available counsel of Mr B.L. Thorne, of Lee, Bolton and Lee, was of inestimable benefit. The Society was associated with the General Synod Board of Education in examining the increasingly serious position on the financing of Church schools, and, with the

Board, produced in 1972 the document, *Crisis in Church Schools*,[5] which advocated coherent diocesan and even national plans for Church Aided schools.

One of the most important developments in the period under review has been the growth of ecumenical co-operation in the educational enterprise. There was increasing consultation with the Roman Catholic Education Council and with the Free Churches. From time to time representatives of these three traditions met for discussion on matters of policy, and the General Secretary was always one of the 'nine'. The results of these consultations were that there was much greater understanding of the *rationale* of involvement in the maintained system, the smoothing out of difficulties over 'single school areas', common approaches to Government on voluntary schools and colleges, and growth also in areas of co-operation in the dioceses, for example Anglican/Roman and Anglican/Methodist schools. It was necessary to steer the Society and the Board of Education through the narrows between politicians on one side and Nonconformist bodies on the other, since there was still what might be called residual suspicion on the part of the Free Churches about Anglican education. Success on both counts characterised in 1959 negotiations on the increase of grant and the possibility of establishing new secondary schools, when Archbishop Fisher wrote to Bishop Stopford, Chairman of the CE Board of Education, as follows:

> I must write to congratulate you, with all my heart on what you have done with Leonard[6] to produce the Government statement on Education. It is really a very fine piece of work not so much for the advantage which it brings to the Church of England, though that is considerable, but for the fact that you have delivered the Churches and the Political Parties from a miserable and unedifying renewal of conflict. It is pleasing to think that the initiative and the leadership all along has, thanks to you, come from the Church of England.

So far as the Church colleges were concerned, it was a story of change, and, alas, in some cases decay. Some colleges closed on the eve of war; others came into existence after the war, particularly during the expansion in the 1960s. St Gabriel's, Camberwell, came under the wing of the Society only to be amalgamated with Goldsmiths' College when the reorganisation of the colleges was undertaken in the early '70s. Berridge House in Hampstead – so long associated with the Society – became a constituent part of All Saints', Tottenham, which itself was later incorporated in a poly-technic. But where colleges were closed, trusts were formed on the proceeds of sale, and so the cause of religious educa-tion was advanced.

In 1953 the Society set out a five-point policy: first, that it maintained the right to express views on religious education; secondly, that it would give full support to Church schools and colleges; thirdly, that it would regard the *content* of religious education as a primary concern; fourthly, that it would continue to manage educational trusts and provide an information service, fifthly, that there would be a register of Church teachers. The first four of these points have provided guidelines for the Society which still obtain, and it can justifiably be claimed that its voluntary character gives strength and independence unhampered by statutory ties to official Church bodies, but with added clout through its staff links with the Synod Board.

The Society has taken a judicious view of developments in religious education (including multifaith problems), as well as a flexible approach to school and college organisation. It has been faithful to its Anglican foundation, yet concerned itself with all education. The publication of the *Durham Report* (1970),[7] the *Carlisle Report* (1971)[8] and *A Future in Partnership* (1984),[9] together with the establishment of RE Centres in Kensington and York, witnesses to this dual duty.

Temple looked forward to a future in partnership. His version has not been unfulfilled; nor has the Society failed to apply its corporate mind to explore the meaning of other words in that Presidential address: 'All true education must be religious in its basis and texture.'

1 William Temple, *The Church Looks Forward,* Macmillan, 1984, page 52
2 Phyllis Dent, *A New Approach to the Church's Work with her Growing Boys and Girls,* National Society, 1938
3 Later Archdeacon; General Secretary of the National Society, 1943-1947
4 *The Church and Education,* Report of the Selborne Commission, Press and Publications Board of the Church Assembly, 1946, page 9
5 *Crisis in Church Schools,* National Society and General Synod Board of Education, 1972

6 Graham Leonard, now Bishop of London and Chairman of the National Society
7 *The Fourth R,* The Durham Report on RE, National Society and SPCK, 1970
8 *Partners in Education:* The Role of the Diocese, Report of the Carlisle Commission, National Society and SPCK, 1971
9 *A Future in Partnership,* National Society, 1984

3
Education and Theology
Stewart Sutherland

Such a title as the one at the head of this essay can misdirect the gaze of our respective expectations. Many of us want to believe, and easily slip into the belief that we inhabit a settled intellectual order in which education is Education and theology is Theology. The specialists in each field have a single and often monochrome vision of the received wisdom and the only stimulus required is towards inter-disciplinary détente where the theological lion will lie down with the educational lamb (or vice-versa to taste). This picture has the added attraction to some theologians of suggesting that they might dispense good advice from their cumulative wisdom to the practitioners in an important field of human activity, in the manner of some of the more traditional treatments of doctrine in which the intellectual direction was always from a foundation in theology proper to the superstructure of something called 'practical' theology.

My opening, and perhaps contentious, affirmation must be that such a picture is a misrepresentation of reality. Indeed I believe that it has never had any status beyond half-informed hopefulness. The relationship between education and theology is a much more complex affair than theologians dispensing theory to practising educationalists. Educational salvation is not to be found in theological edicts.

We are all well aware of the variety of hopes, theories and activities, which can be grouped under the heading 'education'. Whether as pupils, parents or teachers, we have all been in the midst of the ferment of changing precepts and practices in the schools of this country. A central reality of our educational system is a set of deep-seated divergencies over fundamental questions of the aims of the process. Inevitably this shows in differences and changes in the method accepted as appropriate. This is not peculiar to education, for an educational system is in part an expression of the society which it serves and sometimes stings. If within our society there is uncertainty or dissension about goals, then education will share this in great measure. Of course, I do not suggest that there was once a golden age of unanimity and agreement about all things basic, but I do believe that, for a variety of reasons which I cannot expand here, our society is subject to unusually great pressures and tensions. Nor, however, do I accept that pressure and tension are necessarily signs of decay. That remains to be seen. What is clear is that they do mark moments of transition and decision.

Perhaps it is a sense of the impact of all this on education which led the author of the excellent *A Future in Partnership*[1] to point out, doubtless more in sorrow than anger, that

> It seems strange that education, a process which helps to shape the vision humans can have of a particular cultural world and which indicates how personal and communal fulfilment within a particular society might be achieved, has raised relatively little interest among theologians. (page 60)

Indeed it does seem strange, although happily there are some exceptions to the rather bleak and largely correct tenor of this remark.

One of the reasons for this lack of interest must be that theology is in as much difficulty as education. It may be that there is a settled base for theological comment on, in this case, education, but there is little sign that theologians, or for that matter bishops and clergymen, agree on what that base is. Theology, like all Gaul, has been carved up into many parts. The state of theology has become at best federal in nature, though at times civil war seems to be the appropriate metaphor. Of course, even in the time of Paul, there was never a theological monolith but today the situation is significantly different, for reasons which have to do with questions raised by education and its impact on our society. The elucidation of this will be the central theme of this essay.

One temptation which afflicts theologians as much as anyone else shows itself in the priorities set by theologians. It is simply that it is more comfortable to leave the hard questions aside and to proceed where the gradient of intellectual effort is slight. For example, there are few theologians who give to problems of evil and suffering the centrality which they have in the lives of men and women. It is of course rather more easy to hold to such a policy in matters of the mind than in the affairs of the day, though even there procrastination is often a beguiling option. Nonetheless there is an insistence in problems which arise through practice which cannot be set aside or re-ordered as one can with problems of theory. Thus, to continue with the same example, the priest or clergyman cannot defer his response to suffering and evil until a more thorough attention is given to the foundation in exegesis or systematics which reflection on such problems require. The need of the individual parishioner dictates a more urgent timetable.

Education is a matter of practice. As such there will be a peculiar advantage for theology, albeit perhaps a painful one, in engaging in dialogue with or reflection upon the processes of education. Educational practice thrusts upon theologians questions which otherwise and mistakenly they might 'leave till the end'. The nature and range of these questions vary, but each is set in sharp relief by the problems faced in the practice of education, whether pre-school, school, or further and higher education. Each demands a response from theologians and each raises matters of fundamental substance about the very nature of theology itself.

The Response to the Intellectual Roots of Secularism

The importance of this issue for education is sign-posted clearly in *A Future in Partnership*:

> There has been no theological critique of sociology as applied to education. (page 21)

What is being made clear is that there are serious educational questions about the development of thoroughly secular patterns of reflection and their application to school life. To claim this is not to reject such methods, but it is to ask for an independent evaluation of them, and their implicit anthropology (or 'doctrine of man'), from theologians. The development of, effectively, the social sciences, in a context virtually independent of theological reflection, is an example of the dangers of a theological detachment from the world of particular importance for education. Such a charge provides important matter for theological reflection and indicates at the very least a failure of communication between the theologians and the Church (the community of believers). There are three different aspects to this.

(a) At one level the theologians, and the Church at large, are unaware of the implications of the 1870 Education Act which, whatever its faults in providing an adequate public system of education, did set in motion a rapid expansion of a million and a half school places over the next six years. The consequence of this – universal education – has changed the face of our society but there has been remarkably limited grasp of this by theologians and churchmen.

There was a fine grasp of certain aspects of this by ecclesiastical administrators who have served the Church well in the attention which they have paid to the place of Church schools within the state educational system, but the intellectual, and therefore theological, implications have been missed – as have the implications for education in matters of theology and belief.

Undoubtedly many hopes were attached to the 1944 Education Act, and many were happy to assume that this had taken care of all the problems. But the failing of the 1944 Act is that, despite the great sophistication shown by Butler and those with whom he negotiated, it is, in matters religious, intellectually flawed. The sophistication of the Act is political, ecclesiastical and economic. The lack of sophistication is theological and intellectual.

Churchill put his finger on the point when he described the Agreed Syllabus for religious education variously as 'Zoroastrianism' and 'The County Council Creed' – and so it is turning out to be in local education authorities as distant as Birmingham and ILEA. The mistake of the drafters of the act, and even more so of the theologians and Church leaders who failed to challenge this, is that it refused to come to terms with the problems for theology and belief which have been created by the very advance of education within our society which it signalled. In some cases, for example in relation to the concept of authority, these problems extend well beyond religious issues, but more parochially a society in which there is universal education is a society within which the character of belief and theology must be different.

The Butler Act held out the mistaken hope that the problems of theology and religion created by the extension of education could be solved by compulsory school worship and religious instruction for forty minutes each week. The problems, however, are too great for that, for what is overlooked is the immense sophistication which education has brought to every area of human life, and to all of us, whatever our intellectual ability. Thus it is not only the Doctor in Physics, nor the computer specialists, nor the biogeneticists, whose inter-action with the world has increased in complexity. The farm labourer who deals in highly mechanised and clinically sanitised milking processes or complex chemical crop fertilization lives in a world quite unimaginable to his forbears; or the postman who deals with computerised and mechanical mail sorting has expectations from life radically different from those who lived a century ago. Education has been the vehicle of such universal change – education has extended the literary, numerical and scientific skills of *all* of us.

What is noticeably lacking is theological and religious education to match this. There are many reasons for it, including the failure of the state to ensure the supply of, or the local authorities to employ, sufficient trained religious education teachers. Quite apart from that, however, it is apparent that whatever the cause, theologians within the Church, and ecclesiastical leaders, have failed miserably to educate most believers theologically much beyond an elementary Sunday School level. This contrasts with the education which is the foundation of most activities which engage believers throughout their working lives, be they farm-workers, pharmacists or fusion-research specialists.

(b) This leads directly to the second aspect of the growth of secular influences within our society. The Church, and to some considerable extent theology, still have to come to terms with the growth of secular scholarship. The 'Green Paper', *A Future in Partnership* makes honourable mention on a number of occasions of Erasmus. Yet he, as much as anyone, set in train the intellectual problems which still face us. He it was, in his passion for accuracy of text, who made wholehearted application of the techniques of scholarship – literary, textual, linguistic, developed in the study of secular Greek literature – to what was accepted as sacred scripture. Theologians and churchmen are still grappling with the implications of this. The society in which we live, shaped in part by education, is a society in which the methods of humanistic scholarship are taken (if at all), for granted. The study of history, albeit rudimentary in places, is universal.

As the controversy surrounding remarks made by the Bishop of Durham showed well, there is uneasy and unresolved tension within theology and between theologians and Church leaders. The picture becomes even more grave if one notes the superstitious outbursts, given column inches in all areas of the national press, which surrounded the calamitous fire at York Minster in the summer of 1984. I cannot but record that the General Synod missed an opportunity later that year to debate the substantial questions, by formally confining its discussion to the question of what Bishops may and may not say in public. Surely there were much wider and more important questions, for example the role of history in the formation of belief, the need to be clear within the Church about what is true here, and the implications of that for the education of the laity. All of this is central to the question of the theological response to aspects of our society, which in its secular intellectual structure both moulds and is reinforced by our educational system.

(c) The third aspect of this, however, is rather different in tone and points to a positive contribution which theology can make. If one returns to the point made earlier about the need for a theological critique of sociology as applied to education, then I believe the concerns underlying this are plain. The impact of the social sciences upon practice, educational and otherwise, accentuates three intellectual tendencies – relativism, materialism and behaviourism. The first of these is a complex matter and theology's engagement with it is the subject of a growing number of books. However, the second and third in extreme form imply that true understanding of human beings and human societies will be gained by studying only the laws which govern material interactions, and by studying observable behaviour rather than beliefs and emotions, reactions rather than actions.

Such a half-formed ideology can easily distort, for example, educational practice. Materialism and behaviourism go beyond paying proper attention to matter and to behaviour: as 'isms' they would seek to subsume all else under their intellectual domination. To its considerable credit, unlike the physical sciences, the biological sciences, the psychological and social sciences (economics, history and sociology), and the 'educational sciences', monotheistic theology has never even flirted with, let alone espoused, any form of materialism of behaviourism.

To have resisted the 'isms' here is a great tribute and has to do with theology's insistence upon some form of transcendence – some sense of living *sub specie aeternitatis* – if we are to understand ourselves and the world in which we live. This of course must include the exploration of the laws which govern the material world and also the understanding of human behaviour, but it must not thereby subsume and constrict what human beings are. The danger with these 'isms' is that they can *via* practice (educational, social, economic) distort our perception of human beings, and even worse, human beings themselves. Theology has a very important role to play here and educationalists must insist that theologians accept their intellectual responsibilities.

1 Much of my reflection on these topics has been stimulated by
   A Future in Partnership, published by the National Society in 1984.

4

Being Religiously Educated

Basil Mitchell

I want to start from the beginning and ask the prior question whether as educators we should try at all to help the young form some conception of the meaning and purpose of life. Should that be among the aims of school education? Or, should it any longer be?

1. In attempting to answer this question we are confronted at once by the paradox that the very circumstances which might tempt us to answer 'No' press the answer 'Yes' inexorably upon us. The chief reason why we might doubt the propriety of Christian education today is that ours is a society in which there is less agreement than there used to be about the ends of life, and in which it becomes increasingly difficult for the young to take over unreflectively a set of principles which will guide and sustain them. For the more intelligent, at any rate, it is less and less, to use Iris Murdoch's phrase, a matter of 'living in a world' and more and more a matter of 'choosing between worlds'. The extent to which ours is a 'plural society' can be exaggerated, but nevertheless there is a general disinclination to appeal to consideration of a religious or 'philosophical' kind in the expectation of general acceptance. It follows that it is harder to find a warrant in the wider society for a commitment to any positive view of life. And often even families provide a less confident and secure background than they used to.

But this very fact means that growing up can be an alarming and difficult experience, and that help is needed in facing not only the strains of any kind of human life, but the peculiar stresses that come from doubt and insecurity. And my impression is that the 'outside world' is obscurely aware of this and still expects the schools – indeed more than ever expects them – to provide the coherence and conviction which it increasingly lacks. There have, perhaps, been periods when it was unnecessary explicitly to raise questions about the meaning and purpose of life – when certain values were so firmly embedded in the communities people belonged to, and these communities themselves so universally recognized and respected, that there was no need for the individual to raise ultimate questions. People could rely on their moral intuitions and the young could absorb them by a sort of osmosis. But at a time when the chief requirement for a drama or a television documentary is that it should be 'challenging' and 'disturbing' this is no longer the case.

Given the evident need, the tradition of our schools and, indeed, the requirements of law, it is unlikely that we should altogether repudiate the task. But we still have to decide how best to carry it out and, indeed, what more precisely the task is. We are to 'help the young form some conception of the meaning and purpose of life', but how is this to be done?

2. For some time now many educationalists have felt that the only proper way in which to do this is to present to pupils a variety of possible philosophies and equip them with the skills to choose between them. They should not be taught *what* to think, but rather *how* to think. It follows that we should not try to pass on to the young our own beliefs, values and attitudes, but rather encourage them to develop their own. The underlying assumption seems to be that it is possible to equip the average sixteen- to eighteen-year-old with the capacity to understand and evaluate a number of profound and complex systems of belief, together with their moral implications and imaginative expressions, and to do it in such a way that the individual is able to decide which such system of belief should be the formative influence upon his or her life and thought. There are at least three obvious difficulties about this.

(a) The first is that the initial distinction between *what* to think and *how* to think about it cannot be sustained. The only way in which you can teach people how to think is by showing how it is done in practice, and this means taking a serious question and trying to answer it. There may, perhaps, be some very abstract subjects – certain branches of pure mathematics and formal logic – in which it is possible to make a sharp distinction between the principles of reasoning and the matter being thought about, but in most fields of intellectual inquiry it is not. One learns to be an historian, for example, by seeing how a good historian assesses the evidence and arrives at the conclusions he does, and one will not learn this from someone who refuses to come to any conclusions at all.

(b) We learn, as the art historian Ernst Gombrich pointed out in his fascinating book *Art and Illusion,*[1] by a process of schema and correction. We are presented in the first instance with one coherent and intelligible way of organising the phenomena under discussion – and this will normally be the one that our teachers find convincing – and having adopted this, at least provisionally, we then go on to modify it, to re-interpret it and even perhaps, in the end, to reject it altogether.

(c) But, in any case, the systems of belief we are concerned with are not purely intellectual, nor is their importance purely intellectual. They matter because they affect, at the deepest level, our conception of what it is to be a human being. They profoundly affect our emotions, character and attitudes. As Iris Murdoch says:

> We act rightly when the time comes not out of strength of will but out of the quality of our normal attachments and with the kind of energy and discernment which we have available. And to this the whole activity of our consciousness is relevant.[2]

This means, inevitably, that whatever education is given to develop moral, aesthetic and spiritual capacities must to some extent, at least in the early stages, be pre-rational and sub-rational. However much we may have as our ultimate aim a high degree of autonomy, no one can ever achieve it completely, and no-one can even begin to achieve it who has not been reared in a firm tradition in the first place.

There is no way of avoiding responsibility in this matter. If educators scrupulously refrain from exerting any influence or imparting any bias, the young will not thereby be enabled to escape all influence and bias: they will receive the confused imprint of other agencies, most of them less responsible and less scrupulous than the educators themselves.

Perhaps an analogy will serve to illustrate the educator's predicament. Suppose a magic carpet which can learn eventually to vary its own pattern and its own colour, but which from the start is highly responsive to chemicals in the atmosphere. If you leave the carpet untouched it will not remain plain and colourless but will start to assume an appearance that you do not want: either a definite pattern you object to or more probably, if the influences are random ones, a messy and indeterminate appearance. In the latter case, it will never develop its capacity for independent patterning at all. So you have no choice but to select for it at the start the finest pattern you can devise, in the hope that, as it becomes independent of you, it will develop that pattern further in new and exciting ways, which you could not have anticipated. Or suppose a computer which has the capacity to become a creative thinker, but only if it is provided in the first instance with a definite programme which will enable it to develop a distinctive intellectual profile, given which it can start to modify itself in creative ways.

The analogies are not very successful, for the simple reason that to make them credible one has to build into one's description of them the very features which one wants to illustrate and these are uniquely human. But the attempt is, perhaps, worth it if by its very failure it helps us recognize the human situation for what it is. At no stage are human beings totally autonomous, and they are certainly not autonomous when young. We can try not to influence them ourselves, but we cannot prevent them from being influenced at all, nor would it help them if we could.

3. If this is so, and a choice has to be made as to some initial pattern, I do not see that there is any serious alternative to Christianity as the basis of our religious education. Not only has it been the greatest single influence upon our culture, but it continues to touch the lives of many more than those who regularly worship; and even those who reject it still, for the most part, expect to learn from it.

Are we then committed to indoctrination? If our religious education is to be Christian education, must this take the form of inculcating an agreed set of beliefs into a student whose role throughout the process is entirely passive, in such a way as to produce closed minds and restricted sympathies?

Surely not. What we are aiming to do is to introduce people to a tradition, and both the tradition itself and all the people involved in it exhibit enormous variety. Even supposing we were deliberately to select – as in a denominational school we might well wish to do – some particular strand in the Christian tradition, and sought to emphasize that, we should discover that, however successful we were in handing it on, the results would not be uniform. For each individual, in appropriating it, would lend it his own personal colouring, and give it his own individual interpretation and emphasis. If this is true of the taught, it is equally, and importantly, true of the teachers.

Within a tradition – whether religious or any other – conservation and criticism, acceptance and creativity are two sides of one coin. No individual can think up a serious philosophy of life entirely from scratch, and any continuing system of belief becomes ossified if it does not undergo the criticism and inspire the creative imagination of individuals. A religion cannot be summed up definitively in a set of doctrinal formulae (which is not to say that creeds are not necessary). Religious truth is expressed in innumerable ways – in the lives of saints and of ordinary faithful believers, in the liturgy, in painting, architecture, music, and in the reflections of philosophers and theologians; and it is never fully and finally expressed, for 'now we see through a glass darkly, but then face to face'.

Hence to talk, as I have been doing, of 'handing on' all this to the young can by itself be seriously misleading. The metaphor of 'handing on' suggests something manageable, if possible neatly packaged, and preferably not much larger than oneself. Even one's own accumulated understanding of the faith is more than can be adequately expressed in words and, in so far as one can hand on *that*, one hopes that those who receive it will not identify it with the faith itself. The same is true of any kind of teaching. Success consists not in the pupils' being able to reproduce accurately what they have been told, but in their being able to put it in their own words, follow its implications, relate it to other matters, discover fresh problems and so on.

It follows that there is an inevitable tension (in dealing with which the art of the teacher largely consists), between, on the one hand, the need to provide a definite programme of instruction with ample substance and a recognisable shape, and, on the other, the need to activate and inspire the pupil's critical and creative faculties. We come back again, then, to the pattern of schema and correction. Both are necessary. The worry which people are inclined to experience about a religious education which is specifically Christian is that it will be unbalanced and unfair to other points of view. Impartiality, they rightly feel, is essential to anything that is properly called education and impartiality is possible, so they believe, only if the educator himself is neutral. But one does not have to be neutral in order to be impartial. What impartiality does require is that one be fair to an opponent, that one be careful to represent his position in its strongest form, that one look for areas of agreement where that is possible, that one take care not to fudge the argument. But all this is compatible with one's having very firm and definite convictions. Indeed if, in academic life or any other forum, it ever became generally accepted that one could not be impartial without also being neutral, people with definite convictions would feel absolved from any responsibility to be impartial; and that would be the end of all fruitful criticism and debate and all advancement of knowledge.

4. So far, then, I have argued that we ought to try to help the young to find meaning and purpose in their lives; that this may properly involve a commitment to Christian education; and that it must inevitably proceed by way of schema and correction. It is best thought of not as transmitting a completed body of knowledge, but as introducing the young into a living tradition in which the process of schema and correction is going on all the time. But it has to be recognised that this endeavour faces one very serious obstacle today. There is a good deal of evidence that, when children reach the age at which their spiritual capacities begin to develop, there occurs a split between thinking and feeling which affects their capacity to deal with ultimate questions. Thinking is confined to facts which are scientifically demonstrable and are to be expressed in flat, literal language, capable of precise definitions. Everything else – poetry, art, morality, religion – is a matter of feeling and as such belongs to the realm of personal preference, and the language that goes with it is expressive and evocative and makes no claims to truth.

Now there is reason to believe that this cleavage has

been with us for a very long time. As T.S. Eliot remarked in a famous passage: 'In the seventeenth century a dissociation of sensibility set in from which we have never recovered', or as Basil Willey put it in his *Seventeenth Century Background:*

> The cleavage began to appear which has become so troublesomely familiar to us since, between 'values' and 'facts'; between what you *felt* as a human being or a poet, and what you *thought* as a man of sense, judgement and enlightenment.[3]

Hence it often happens that people make up their minds about religion once and for all in their early teens and never *think* about it again. They either accept or, more frequently, reject a version of Christianity which is understood with a kind of flat literalness more appropriate to scientific fact than to spiritual understanding – and not very appropriate even to that. So understood, it remains on the surface of the mind and, if it is not eventually cast off, serves as an impermeable layer of lifeless matter through which deeper spiritual impulses cannot penetrate. So one gets acceptance or rejection of a kind of religious belief which is a sort of mirror-image of naive scientism itself – or, instead, highly personal religious feelings which are genuine enough but cannot draw upon the intellectual and imaginative resources of a historical tradition or undergo testing by reference to it.

5. What can be done about it?

a) The problem is not one of religious teaching only, but also of science teaching, and this suggests strongly that the two need to be brought together in some way. The times are propitious for doing it; there is an increasing emphasis in the philosophy of science both on the limitations of scientific method and on the role of the imagination in scientific work. Scientists are for the most part much less ready than they used to be even a short time ago to limit the domain of knowledge to scientific knowledge, and more aware of the part played *in* scientific thinking itself by the choice of models and by the scientist's personal judgement.

b) On the religious side a sustained attempt has to be made to prevent the disastrous split from occurring, which means feeding the imagination on images, symbols and parables which are expressed through liturgy, prayer, drama, poetry and fiction, music and the visual arts; and at the same time encouraging critical reflection upon the entire tradition which they represent. It is hard to see how such a programme can be carried through by religious specialists alone. Indeed, the cultural split in question is a threat not only to religious studies but also to the study of history, literature and the arts, indeed to all the disciplines whose basic subject matter is human thoughts, feelings, intentions and purposes, and which therefore have an interest in preventing the impoverishment of language and in maintaining its capacity to express different sorts of truth.

c) The vital transition that has to be made emotionally, imaginatively, ethically, intellectually occurs, if it occurs at all, at an age when the young are peculiarly unsure of themselves and anxious about their own identity. Two things follow from this. One is that the ethos of the school is all-important. There needs to be a firm framework, which supports without crushing the individual; in which the young by being valued can come to value themselves rightly. In a community which must value academic standards there is a constant temptation to judge people by their ability to satisfy them, and to forget that most fundamental of Christian insights: that we are to love people not on account of their qualities but for their own sakes. (This does not, of course, mean that we should not mind what they make of themselves: that would be indifference, not love). It goes without saying that, if a school claims to be Christian and does not preponderantly express this truth in its dealings with its members, its Christian witness will fail: the young will experience a contradiction, and they will lack the sort of confidence in themselves and their mentors which is needed if they are to make this difficult transition successfully.

The other is that at every stage in the process the school should observe a certain restraint. Although religious belief is not simply an expression of individual preference, it *is* deeply personal and must, in the end, be a matter of genuinely free choice. People need a private spiritual space - perhaps especially in adolescence; and this means that there should be no excessive emotional or intellectual pressure exercised by the institution as such. Hence both in worship and in classroom teaching, except where the former is entirely voluntary, the attempt to secure commitment is, I believe, out of place. No serious induction into a religious tradition could fail to make it clear that, sooner or later, commitment is involved. But during this difficult and sensitive stage of adolescence what we need to ensure is that the young are given the resources for making a decision in their own time rather than required to make it prematurely. There is a passage in the writings of the late Professor H.H. Price which contains a great deal of wisdom on this matter. It occurs towards the end of his monumental Gifford Lectures on *Belief:* he is talking about the Gospel narratives:

> The important thing is not that we should believe these narratives, or how firmly we believe them, if we do. What is recommended is that we should think of them assiduously and attentively, think over them and ruminate upon them . . . We may also believe these (religious) propositions or some of them, but the important thing is that we should be *interested* in them, interested enough to try to realize fully what their content is and to let our thoughts dwell on them. If we believe them without being interested in them, and without any tendency at all to ruminate over them or meditate upon them, we cannot expect that this will have much effect in developing spiritual capacities. What we think about, privately and inwardly, and think about often, is much more important from this point of view than what we believe, and much more likely to alter our personalities. Belief can come later.[4]

The observance of restraint with respect to commitment is entirely compatible with the school's making clear where it stands and with the individual teacher's not disguising his or her own convictions. Once this is recognised the approach to Christian education I have been commending can and should take over much of the practice characteristic of the phenomenological approach.

Price's insight enables us, in conclusion, to answer one unavoidable question about our religiously educated people: to be 'religiously educated' must they be committed Christians? For if they were familiar with the Christian story and meditated upon it, so that their imaginations had been touched by it and their characters formed by it, and if they had reflected critically upon it and knew what was at stake in the acceptance or rejection of it, above all if they knew how much more there was to learn, then they would be religiously educated. If need be, 'belief can come later'.

1. Ernst Gombrich, *Art and Illusion*, Phaidon, 1960
2. Iris Murdoch, *The Sovereignty of Good*, Routledge Kegan Paul, 1970, page 92
3. Basil Willey, *Seventeenth Century Background*, Chatto & Windus, 1934, page 294
4. H.H. Price, Gifford Lecture, *Belief*, George Allen & Unwin, 1969, page 478

Graham Leonard, Bishop of London and Chairman of the National Society.
© KEITH ELLIS, ARPS

National Society officers outside Church House, Westminster.
Back row: Colin Alves (General Secretary), Geoffrey Duncan (Deputy Secretary), Ian Pearson (Archivist). Centre: David Maudlin (Administration and Finance Officer). Front: Joanna Yates (Promotions and Publications Secretary), Pat Heaven (Personal Assistant to the General Secretary).
PHOTOGRAPH: TREVOR HUMPHRIES

The old building which, with additions, is still in use.

Penley School Gardens.

Boys working in the school gardens, 1912.

Mr Martindale's class, 1912.

The Madras School, Penley, near Wrexham. Founded in 1811; the oldest school in Wales associated with the National Society.

The National Junior School, Grantham. Founded in 1812; the building dates from 1859.

PHOTOGRAPH: C KIDD

The Bishop of London visiting a Church primary school: St John's, Friern Barnet.

A classroom at St Audries School, West Quantoxhead. Founded in 1906, presented to the Church of England in 1944 and held in trust by the National Society.

The College of St Mark and St John, Plymouth. A National Society foundation; the College moved from London to Plymouth in 1973.

Students examining the resources at the National Society's RE Development Centre, Kensington.

PHOTOGRAPH: TREVOR HUMPHRIES

Students at Trinity College, Carmarthen, a National Society foundation dating from 1848.

PHOTOGRAPH: JOHN HARRIS

5

Curriculum for the Future

David Hargreaves

For over a decade the curriculum of the secondary school has been under review. This debate was an inevitable result of the re-organisation of secondary education along comprehensive lines. Prime Minister Callaghan's famous Ruskin College speech of 1976 is often held to be the main instigator of the debate, but this unusual prime ministerial intervention in educational affairs was a sensible attempt to pre-empt Conservative critics of comprehensive schooling. In so doing James Callaghan formally drew attention to an issue which hitherto had not been sufficiently acknowledged, namely the secondary school curriculum. Support for the comprehensive school had been won on the basis of an ideology of extending educational opportunities for all (or, as Harold Wilson had so skilfully expressed it, 'grammar schools for all'), which traded upon the unpopularity of the eleven-plus rather than the virtues of the comprehensive school as such. In consequence, the curriculum of the comprehensive school was treated as unproblematic: it was to be the grammar school curriculum. The experience of many secondary modern schools, that a watered-down academic curriculum was in many ways unsuitable for many of their pupils, was ignored. The fact that many of the top streams in secondary modern schools had followed a grammar school curriculum and succeeded in public examinations was sufficient to suppress a crucial question: what curriculum is appropriate for a comprehensive school and to what areas of the curriculum are *all* pupils entitled?

Today we are closer to an answer. In the Inner London Education Authority, the curricular recommendations of *Improving Secondary Schools* (1984),[1] which are very close to the later suggestions of the Secretary of State, Sir Keith Joseph, have been accepted. These propose that the curriculum should, in the words of HMI, be 'broad, balanced and coherent'. In particular, the recommendations mark a move away from a rather small 'core curriculum' of compulsory subjects in the fourth and fifth years (usually English, mathematics, physical education and religious education) plus a large, and usually complex, set of options, towards a much larger core with reduced options. *Improving Secondary Schools* recommended the following compulsory subjects in the fourth and fifth years: English, mathematics, science, personal and social education (PSE) with religious education (RE), at least one arts subject (art, music, dance or drama), and at least one technical subject (such as craft, design and technology (CDT) or computer studies). Humanities (history and geography), languages (classical or modern) and physical education were, somewhat controversially to some, assigned to the optional category.

Now it can be argued that this is a very backward-looking approach to the curriculum of the comprehensive school. First, it is fairly close to the grammar school curriculum, even though the humanities and languages now become optional rather than compulsory. Secondly, it is conceived in terms of the conventional disciplines or subjects, each of which is insulated from the others. Thirdly, it preserves the existing status hierarchy of knowledge, with English and mathematics in a position of unchallenged pre-eminence. It is thus very far from being a radical curriculum change, even though this seems to be demanded by the substantial disenchantment of many young people in comprehensive schools and by the need to prepare them more adequately for the future in a rapidly changing society.

If a radical curriculum requires an almost complete break with the curriculum of the past, the objections are valid. However, I want to argue that we are in a period of very fundamental curriculum change, and this process will not be helped by the creation of a radical curriculum – whatever that might look like. Effective curriculum development and change, I contend, will come by a process of evolution, rather than of revolution, or a sudden and dramatic departure from the past. There are several reasons for this. We do not, in fact, have available to us many examples of a 'radical curriculum' and certainly none that commands widespread agreement. Moreover, we do not know what the curriculum demands will be in, say, the year 2000; since both society and knowledge are changing very fast, we must be very flexible in our approach to the curriculum. Evolution allows flexibility; revolution will more likely engender what would soon become a new conservatism. In any event, most teachers could not cope with a curricular revolution: they need to develop and change from where they now are, adapting with confidence and preserving the best of the past. Even if teachers could indeed cope with more radical change, the power of the examination boards on sixteen-plus examinations is such that real curricular change is inevitably rather slow.

The proposed curriculum has within itself the seeds of substantial change through its potential for evolution. Two changes mark a distinct departure from the traditional academic curriculum of the grammar school. In the grammar school curriculum, technical subjects usually meant woodwork and/or metalwork (largely for boys), and these studies were usually made optional, especially for 'academic' pupils after the third year. One effect has been the high status accorded to the 'pure' sciences and low status accorded to applied science and technology, including engineering. We continue to pay a heavy price for this poor investment in technological skills. The arts, like technology, were assigned a lowly position in the grammar school curriculum. Making at least one of the arts compulsory in the fourth and fifth years restores the arts to their rightful place as an equal with English, mathematics, science, technology, and personal and social education. Since the Gulbenkian Report on *The Arts in Schools* (1982) there has been an enhanced understanding of value of the arts in the curriculum. In 1977 HMI named 'the spiritual' as one of the eight 'areas of experience' which ought to be covered by the secondary school curriculum, and it is perhaps significant that they do not see this as entirely co-terminous with the religious or the ethical. For many people the arts are one of the most important roads to the spiritual domain, and in this sense the arts are a significant ally of religious education. The links between the spiritual, the aesthetic and the religious are evident in the Church's liturgy and should warn us against a religious education that is in danger of becoming too exclusively cognitive. In the same way, some understanding of religion is essential to a proper appreciation of so much of Western art, music, drama and poetry.

The new curriculum, then, is certainly more broad and balanced than the old grammar school curriculum; but is it more *coherent*? This last concept suggests that the curriculum should be more than a collection of subjects: the curriculum *as a whole* should 'hang together' and have collective meaning in the experience and life of the pupils. Because the new comprehensive school curriculum remains a list of separate subjects, there is a real danger that coherence will not be achieved. Coherence demands that we make connections between different subjects or parts of the curriculum, and too often in our schools even the most basic connections are sadly lacking. It is still relatively rare, for example, for the teachers of science, mathematics and CDT to plan their syllabuses in such a way that pupils see real links between these three curriculum areas and acquire knowledge and skills in one subject at a time and in a form which facilitates their deployment in one of the other two subjects. At a higher level, each subject should consciously see itself as a bridge between curriculum areas. CDT, for instance, is at its best a bridge between art and design on the one hand, and science and mathematics on the other. Only when all subjects see themselves as agents of integration of the curriculum as a whole can we justifiably claim that we are tackling the problem of curriculum coherence. It is this coherent curriculum which is now in process of evolution.

In advocating a place for personal and social education (PSE) in the compulsory curriculum of the fourth and fifth years, *Improving Secondary Schools* was making another break with the past. For PSE is not a subject or discipline: it is a curriculum area. Indeed, there is as yet no generally agreed definition of PSE. It includes areas which are often taken to be separate subjects, such as careers education or health education, both of which have, happily, gained in importance with the rise of the comprehensive school. But it also includes capacities and skills, such as study skills, which are truly cross-curricular. Other components have no generally agreed disciplinary base. Political education may belong to history or social studies, but is not necessarily covered by either; the mass media may, or may not, be dealt with in English lessons: consumer education and education for parenthood and family life have often been well handled by teachers of home economics, but this subject is not by any means always taken by older pupils, especially boys; community service and community studies sometimes form an important part of religious education or social studies, but too often this is seen as appropriate for 'less able' pupils only. PSE, then, is an interdisciplinary area to which many, perhaps all, subjects should contribute: it has enormous integrative potential if – and it is a considerable if – teachers accept this potential and are willing to devote time and energy to it.

Improving Secondary Schools proposed that in the third to fifth years of secondary education, the curriculum should be designed in the form of half-term *units,* and that each unit should result in a *credit,* or record of what had been achieved within each unit. It was recognised that, at least in the first instance, most units would be within subjects, and as such might not contribute to curricular coherence. But it was hoped that within each subject there might be units which forged explicit links with other subjects. In science, for instance, as well as units in physics, chemistry and biology and units which integrated the three traditional disciplines, there might also be a few units which strove for links with other subjects. A unit on food science could link biology and chemistry with home economics; a unit on the earth sciences with geography; a unit on medicine with health education; and so on. This is a very practical way in which the seeds of considerable curriculum development can be sown.

Religious education has an opportunity within this changed approach to a new curriculum. It is a distinct subject or discipline, and fortunately parents continue to demand that it should be taught within our schools. But in pupils' estimations it continues to be one of the least popular subjects. In the supportive research done for *Improving Secondary Schools* RE was seen by pupils as the least useful and the most boring subject. It is a subject in which, from the pupil point of view, there is the greatest demand for change. Yet many RE teachers remain curiously conservative and afraid of change;

many cling to their (usually small) examination classes among older pupils and lose sight of the needs of pupils who either are not taking a public examination or who do not like the subject when they are. Of course RE teachers in maintained schools have reasons to feel defensive. Status tends to go to teachers with successful examination classes and some headteachers are frankly unsympathetic to the subject with the result that the RE department is inadequately staffed, and can become suddenly vulnerable in a period of falling rolls and of a shortage of appropriately qualified RE teachers.

RE is not the only subject to feel threatened during this period of curriculum change: modern languages, history and geography are less secure than they were, and they lack the legal backing of the 1944 Act which buttresses RE. Whether RE teachers will respond positively to the challenges presented by new curriculum remains to be seen, but there are certainly many opportunities. As we move towards a modular and more coherent curriculum, RE should enter into alliances with other subjects: as suggested above, the spiritual area of experience can be a basis for new units or modules with arts subjects. RE has much to contribute to the humanities, as integrated humanities courses in the first three years of secondary school have demonstrated when the RE specialist plays a part equal to that of the geographer or historian. There are ample opportunities for the RE specialist to contribute to cross-curricular units or modules in the fourth or fifth years. *Improving Secondary Schools* believed there to be a particularly strong link between PSE and RE. A PSE course would be seriously deficient without RE. On the other hand RE cannot be reduced to, or entirely subsumed by, PSE. It will not be easy to avoid these twin dangers, but an RE which refuses to take any risks and defensively maintains itself as a completely separate and distinctive subject is likely to remain unpopular with pupils and to find itself increasingly isolated from the important curricular changes which are leading to much improved whole curriculum planning. Hitherto Church schools have a poor record in showing how an imaginatively designed and out-going RE can take the lead towards whole curriculum coherence. Is it unreasonable to expect that Church schools should be exemplars of how the new curriculum for the future does not merely include RE but uses RE to spearhead coherent whole curriculum planning?

Should not these schools be giving a stronger lead in demonstrating the value of an RE-based PSE? It is, at least to me, ironical that Christianity, a religion which pervades the whole of our living and being, should have been so slow, in its educational expression, to pervade the whole of the curriculum.

Such a religious education would make great demands on RE teachers. Already we are finding in the ILEA, with our newly agreed multifaith syllabus, that many RE teachers are not well trained for these new demands on their knowledge and their teaching skills, even though it is recognised that the new syllabus has much to contribute to multicultural and anti-racist education in the inner city. The education and teacher training of the RE specialist, including later in-service training, is in urgent need of review. A sound theological training, even in religions in addition to Christianity, is not enough, for the curriculum pioneers of the future require not only specific disciplinary expertise but also a much broader understanding of the whole curriculum and its various components.

The Church has taken the educational lead in the past; it is part of our national history in which we can take pride. The educational challenge to the Church, and to the powerful role still played by the Church in higher education and teacher education, has changed very considerably. If religious education in the next generation and the curriculum of the future are to be worthy of their inheritance, then the Church will need to devote more time, imaginative thought and costly resources to religious education and its under-valued specialist teachers. Leadership, in this matter as in all others, requires vision, confidence and commitment. Is the Church providing them?

1. *Improving Secondary Schools*, Inner London Education Authority, 1984

6
Education in Worship
John Gwinnell

'What is worship?' jesting Pilate might more appropriately have asked, for worship has so many facets that generalisation is dangerous and trivialisation all too common in schools. The variety of worship within any one tradition is also considerable and, whether in 1986 or in 1811, worship in schools is certain to vary in accordance with the whims of headteachers and clergy.

Our link with 1811 should be in the expectation that, now as then, the experience of worship will inspire and instruct, elevate and enlighten the worshippers. Doubtless those who framed the 1944 Education Act and its provision for the daily act of worship hoped that the young would be suitably enlightened; nor is such an expectation unreasonable, for spiritual experience is not an optional extra in anyone's life and young people show a natural gift for worship. Today the sources of inspiration are widened beyond the Christian scriptures that were the staple diet in 1811, but to share with the receptive minds of youngsters that which mankind has found inspiring and enriching remains part of the educational enterprise.

Common prayer or corporate worship is not easy to organise in school communities that are more varied and cosmopolitan than ever they were. Christian schools can properly offer Christian worship, and that will include offering the whole life of the school – the curriculum. It remains true that any school can celebrate the curriculum and seek to share that which its members corporately believe has worth in the life of the school. Her Majesty's Inspectors, in their document on the *Curriculum, 11-16*,[1] specifically include the spiritual development of pupils among their concerns. It would be unreasonable for any school or LEA to deprive children of spiritual experience or of their religious heritage. It is part of the affirmative role of the school to enable pupils to take part in school worship and make their particular contribution. Young people are often prepared to devote much time and thought and energy to excellence in worship. They also need opportunity to express their aspirations, their hopes and their concerns, though they may do so with a directness and simplicity that adults find shocking or inspiring or both at once.

It will be an important part of the corporate life of the school for different age groups and interest groups to share what they have to offer. Assemblies for worship which are a genuine focus for the whole life of the school will make no artificial distinctions between the sacred and the secular. Praise for a sporting achievement or concern about litter will be a part of such worship as, crucially, will the involvement of staff and pupils in a genuinely corporate activity.

Robert Waddington, formerly General Secretary of the National Society, in his 1985 Hockerill Lecture referred to 'the bewildering mixture of doubt and faith that forms so much of our religious journeying'.[2] Any school will contain staff and pupils at different stages of their personal pilgrimage. Few will want to or be able to say 'Amen' to everything that takes place in school worship. The school must in any case respect the religious freedom of the individual. It cannot, however, opt out of the responsibility to enrich the spiritual experience of its members or of enabling them to share what others have found inspiring and of eternal worth.

Church schools have a particular responsibility and opportunity to aim at excellence in school worship. We shall not always succeed: sometimes pupils (and staff) will yawn; standards will vary, but the fundamental importance of worship will not be in doubt. The Allington statement of June 1981 expressed this unequivocally in asserting that Church schools 'have the example of Jesus Christ as the fundamental source of inspiration'.[3]

Within Church schools there will be striving after the will of God, a recognition of the plural nature of society and regular participation in and contribution to worship and the sacramental life. The fruits of the Spirit will be evident in the life of the school: such are love, joy, peace, patience, gentleness, goodness, faith, meekness, temperance. The school will collectively affirm God as Creator and Jesus Christ as Saviour, belief in the divine nature of a purpose for man, and the glory of all created things.

The practical working-out of school worship will inevitably produce wide variations, and there is no doubt that a great deal of imaginative Christian worship takes place in our Church schools, both primary and secondary. It would be pointless to try to generalise about how Church schools are using the opportunities that are theirs. I can only describe how we tried to reflect some of the splendours of worship in one school, and gratefully acknowledge the contribution of the head of RE and of the clergy, as well as of everyone else involved.

We gather together to make explicit what is implicit in the life of the school and to respond to God in praise and love. Planning at least a term in advance is essential. Themes such as the way five faiths use the symbol of light require detailed, skilled preparation. A worship committee can talk over material, approach staff, meet groups of pupils, invite speakers and, perhaps most important, communicate how available time is ordered for particular ingredients. Pupils will refer to fun, laughter, silence, caricature, space, embarrassment, time-span, language, leadership, boredom in intensely practical ways. We should listen, for they are often wise. Where services may occur in Church, then a year's programme is needed and must go on the school calendar early.

Reverence can rarely be quantified, though it is qualitatively sensed. Variety, flexibility, clarity, simplicity, (not the same as patronising an 18 year old to make sense to the 12 year old) humanity, joy can all be planned for. Relevance is an overused word but if what adults dictate (young people rarely make this mistake) is 'unrelated to children's awareness of society, science, human relationships, work or leisure it will be rejected'.[4]

Leadership is crucial. Tact, patience, persuasion, facilitating, supportiveness are as important as inspiration and imagination. The head of religious education may or may not be the right person to co-ordinate the planning; the head-teacher will rarely be so. Participation by staff and by pupils has been stressed. Most pupil groups will require the aid of adult skills of refinement and presentation. Staff/pupil joint ventures are often exciting but individual teacher presenta-tions may suffer from reliance on personal charisma which obscures rather than enlightens.

Relaxed, well-ordered presentation often achieves more rapt attention than the intense and the domineering. One can almost hear Jesus say 'I want to tell you a story'. 'Laid-back' is perhaps an appropriate phrase if we avoid the connotations of casualness or emptiness. Curiosity is in us all. One can reach the position where many children and many staff wonder 'What's in store for us today?' in a positive, anticipatory way. This does not imply a resort to gimmickry but rather an expectation of imaginative effort.

The use of art, music, drama and a variety of audio and visual aids is now commonplace. They complement and do not displace the Bible, the written word from other sources, prayer and quietness. Balance is needed between what is familiar and what is new; between the reassuring and the disturbing; the salving and the painful, or, as Robert Waddington puts it, 'handling the intermediate area of experience between potential separation of belief and doubt, of truth and falsehood, – of success and failure, of the knowledge of God and of the mystery he is'.[5] There will be risks since 'how can we be Christian with our children if we live as men and women who have arrived, for children of all folk perceive the riskiness, promise and adventure of a world yet to be fulfilled'.[6] Neither school life nor its gathering to worship has a purpose to proselytise. We are not in the busi-ness of turning out cardboard Christians or of filling pews.

So what is success? I cannot say. One child may sense God alongside or the whole community may radiate grace. We offer, God gives. At St Edward's School, Romford we offered an opportunity for communal worship, usually at 3.20 pm (with no other competition for time) through a gathering of the whole school twice weekly and age groups meeting separately once a week. On Friday afternoon the week is gathered together. Termly Eucharists in school for year groups are complemented by informal lunchtime

Eucharists for senior pupils and staff. Services in school and at its 'family' churches are held on a termly basis and at Christmas and Easter. Passover feasts, services of other faiths led by their priests, a formal God-speed to leavers, and staff Eucharist at the start of year, represent a variety owing much to colleagues and to the Vicar of Romford. There are many visitors, much noise and quite a lot of fun. Once we listened to a tape of a class in progress amidst shelling in a Christian school in Beirut; months later Mohammed and his friends from that classroom came to us. A storm followed by dramatic calm on Galilee was an experience shared by a party who visited the Holy Land. We roared with laughter at Christians caricaturing their own foibles and prejudices, and chuckled with a teacher recounting an eventful cycle tour of Greece and his consequent growth in understanding of prayer. We watched a Franciscan 'strip' to show the ordinary human beneath the habit and heard the apologia of the Greenham Common protester. There was the dramatic occasion when an enthusiastic teacher graphically portrayed the prancing white horses at the Day of Judgement and the visiting curate arose in a fury to denounce the heresy; what an opportunity for reconciliation and understanding that turned out to be.

The whole approach may be thought naive. I am not scholar enough to defend it theologically, but there is some living evidence that it works. Even if formal homage in the often intended sense is infrequent, then the shared fun, sorrow, achievements, learning, praise, all in God's name will be joyfully accepted as part of the search and commitment of a community of people who are all *Just Young*[7] in faith and understanding.

1 *Curriculum 11-16*, Department of Education and Science, HMSO, 1977
2 Robert Waddington, *The Unknown, Remembered Gate*, Hockerill Educational Foundation Lecture, 1985
3 The Allington Statement, published June 1981 by a group of Church School Headteachers and reprinted almost in full in *A Future in Partnership*, National Society, 1984, page 54
4 *A Task for all Christians*, Chelmsford Diocesan Council for Education and Training, 1982
5 Robert Waddington, *op. cit.*
6 *Ibid.*
7 *Just Young*, edited by Patrick Appleford, Chelmsford Diocesan Council for Education and Training, 1984

7
Church Schools: Present and Future
Geoffrey Duncan

The Church's involvement in education, including institutional provision, has a long history. Implicit within the current all-embracing question *What On Earth Is The Church For?*,[1] is the specific question 'Is the Church "for" Church schools?'. This issue, not for the first time, engenders controversy both within and outside the Church. Not so many years ago one observer commented that 'during the 1960s controversy about the relations between Church and State in the field of education continued to diminish'.[2] The 1980s, however, are showing signs that the controversy is recurring.[3] Latent and sometimes open opposition or criticism has been accompanied by the present government's proclaimed support for voluntary schools[4] but it should not be assumed that all Conservative central and local politicians are so committed. In any case it cannot be in the interests of voluntary schools for their cause to become identified with one particular political party. Certainly the Church of England could benefit from having more Labour and Alliance Members of Parliament willing to speak in support of its schools. (The Roman Catholics seem to do better in this regard.) The words of Murphy are salutary: ' . . . there is hesitation and doubt in Church circles about future policies; and it may be that in the next hundred years the problems for the Churches in educational work will be such as cannot be solved by assistance, however generous, from the State'.[5] The next decade or two will probably provide sufficient challenges to encourage (or force) the Church to resolve its doubts and uncertainties about its schools.

Church Schools: Present –

When A.J. Balfour introduced the 1902 Education Bill, he provided statistics which showed that over 71 per cent of schools were voluntary. In January 1985[6] 21 per cent of schools were voluntary, the Church of England share being as follows*:

Total of all primary schools (including middle deemed primary)	=	19716
No. of C E aided primary schools	—	1964
No. of C E controlled primary schools	—	2911
No. of C E special agreement schools	—	1
Total of all secondary schools (including middle deemed secondary)	—	4382
No. of C E aided secondary schools	—	119
No. of C E controlled secondary schools	—	101
No of C E special agreement schools	—	18
Total no. of all schools	=	24098
Total no. of C E schools	=	5114

The statistics of the last three decades reveal one significant factor: that during the period 1950-1984, when there was a 14 per cent reduction in all primary schools, there was a 42 per cent reduction in the number of Church of England primary schools. The main explanation is that the majority of small schools were (and continue to be) Church of England schools. A Culham Occasional Paper[7] has drawn attention to the implications of this, particularly in the light of the Government White Paper *Better Schools,* and to the challenge before 'both the Church and the LEAs in their joint work in partnership to provide the most effective and sensible pattern of education for young children currently in small primary schools'.[8]

---

*Throughout much of this essay no distinction is drawn between aided, controlled and special agreement schools, except where the difference in status seems relevant. This is to make the point that Church of England controlled schools are Church schools, although there are different opinions and practices as to the strength of the Church connection. (See page 76 for an explanation of the difference between aided, controlled and special agreement schools).

Expediency would appear at least sometimes to help the work of the Holy Spirit, in so far as falling rolls, closures and re-organisations have encouraged at least some of the growing number of 'joint schools' – Anglican/Methodist and Anglican/Roman Catholic* – and some have been in operation long enough for more positive Christian motivation than expediency to flourish. The Christian Church must still be a puzzle if not a scandal to some LEAs who maintain in some small villages both a small Church of England and a small Roman Catholic school yet perceive one strong, viable joint school as an obvious answer to some of their problems. An even greater scandal to the Church of England is that Churchmanship can still significantly obtrude: in one English city this factor adversely affected the possibility of the amalgamation of two small aided C of E secondary schools to form one strong, viable school. The Church might now lose both!

A National Society poster some years ago proclaimed 'Church and School – Heart of the Village Community'. In the inner city, too, as recalled by the Rev. Harry Williams, a Church school could help bind the parish into a community.[9] An increasing number of Church schools now find such a cosy identification of church, community and school less and less applicable, particularly where multifaith and multicultural factors exist.[10] There is no one model to commend for a Church school in such a setting, but if ad hoc, piecemeal and sometimes confused reactions to new situations are to be avoided, the Church at many levels needs in a co-ordinated and consistent way to do much more to help guide and support the governing bodies of Church schools. Aided school governors in particular, with their responsibility for staff appointment, admissions, religious education and worship, often have to make difficult decisions. Raising the right questions is doubtless an essential stage, but it is time the Church through its various agents offered more in the way of a range of possible answers or responses. There is at least one Church aided school without a single Christian child and a growing number where children of other faiths,

---

*There are at the time of writing 5 joint Anglican/Roman Catholic aided secondary schools and one primary. There are 25 joint Anglican/Methodist schools (aided and controlled).

sometimes with Muslims in the majority, predominate. At least one governing body of such a Church school has declared to the Secretary of State its unwillingness to continue with aided status. This raises at least two fundamental questions: should it be possible for a governing body to make such an irrevocable decision about the Church's provision of schools and is it really impossible or inadvisable to evolve and propagate a role and policy for a Church school in such circumstances rather than for the Church to pull out? One Church school that does so far see a role for a Church aided school serving a majority of Muslim pupils has three Muslim governors (two of whom are foundation governors!). One example of good practice recently provided by this school was to have a two-day closure for in-service training at which staff and governors sought to understand more about the school's role and work towards a model to which all contributed and which all can largely affirm and support.

Church schools in other settings can become a little impatient with what they see as too great a preoccupation with the multicultural scene. An article posing challenges to Church schools in a multicultural setting[11] drew the response that many Church schools in rural areas, unaffected by multi-faith factors, also have serious challenges to face, not least the size of school and threat of closure issues.[12] Whilst this point has to be accepted, even such schools are enjoined to consider an appropriate *Education for All* in a pluralist society unless the central thesis of the Swann Report is to be rejected.[13]

What is distinctive about Church schools, whether or not they serve a multifaith area? Answers frequently confuse prescriptive statements with descriptive statements; in other words, when people offer what they think *is* distinctive about a church school they are often really saying what *ought* to be distinctive. At a meeting of aided school headteachers in one diocese a couple of years ago, one speaker (a LEA Inspector) suggested that the crunch question was not so much 'What are Church Schools For?' as 'What do Church Schools Do?' Answers by Church people often revolve around the special 'ethos' of a Church school – at times an elusive, indefinable creature – or the priority given to religious education and worship. On the latter point, one recent report suggests no grounds for complacency: 'There is a surprisingly large number of (Church) primary schools which do not appear to have a clear policy on RE.'[14] On the question of ethos all Church schools should ponder the comments in *A Future in Partnership* on this matter: 'Ethos cannot be left to chance: it must be thought about and patterns of action tried and assessed.'[15] This is a vital activity for everyone involved in the community of a Church school. One way of helping Church schools rise to this challenge and other present and future ones is to make greater efforts to disseminate good practice. There is a tendency only for the failures and deficiencies of Church schools to be publicised. More could be done to share challenges, opportunities, difficulties and ways of responding to them. The gratified reactions of participants in national conferences, for example, for Heads of Church of England secondary schools and for Church schools with a significant number of Muslim pupils, organised by the General Synod Board of Education and the National Society, have provided striking testimony to the potential for binding Church schools closer together.

Quite simply the Church in some respects often knows very little about what actually goes on in its Church schools. As the Bishop of London has written in the preface to a recently published book, 'It can be very easy erroneously to assume that one has an adequate grasp of both the past and the present scene throughout the country.'[16] He goes on to stress the value of local studies. Concerned with the attitudes of teachers in aided and controlled schools in one particular diocese, the book highlights a crucial area for study because one possible answer to what can make a Church school distinctive lies in the commitment of the staff – their commitment to a set of beliefs and values and their commitment to their school as a *Church* school. The study suggests, however, that teachers in Church schools are often uncertain or ambivalent in their attitudes to working in Church schools. This reveals considerable scope for efforts by the National Society/General Synod Board of Education/Dioceses/Parishes/Governors to help staff – whatever their original motivation for seeking their appointment – to adopt a more positive attitude to their Church school.

The appointment of teaching staff in present circumstances poses a dilemma for the partnership with LEAs. With falling pupil rolls governors of aided schools are frequently asked to consider appointing to a vacancy a teacher (who may not be an Anglican or even a Christian) redeployed from a County school. The staff of an aided school helps to make such a school distinctive (and if Church schools are not distinctive, why have them?), yet in the spirit of co-operation and concern that teachers should not be declared redundant, governors have often rightly accepted such redeployed teachers. (It also of course works the other way – displaced Church school teachers being redeployed to County schools.) Perhaps as numbers stabilise this complication will recede, though Church schools will still be faced with the challenge of recruiting teachers who have positive reasons for wishing to work in them.

With other schools in the maintained system Church schools have been reconstituting their governing bodies to meet the requirements of the 1980 Education Act. As with staff, foundation governors could and should be a source from which Church schools derive a distinctive character. Yet this is another area about which comparatively little is known: how are Church of England school foundation governors recruited, selected, trained and supported? One of the features of Church school governing bodies is the ex-officio status as a governor of the incumbent (or 'principal officiating minister', to use the legal term). Furthermore, it still tends to be the rule rather than the exception that the incumbent becomes chairman of the governing body. Where this near-automatic relationship works well it is a great and obvious benefit to the school. Where it does not work well the effect on the school, equally obviously, can be disastrous. These observations prompt various questions: to what extent do patrons of livings bear in mind the Church school when considering appointing a priest to the parish – or how easy or likely is it for someone to be appointed with no interest in or suitability for the post of ex-officio foundation governor? What, if any, initial training (pre- and post-ordination) is given to prepare the clergy for undertaking the very responsible role of chairman of a school governing body? Until and unless the Church gives more attention to questions such as these, so on the one hand the potential for a creative relationship redounding to the credit of Church schools is compromised and, on the other hand, the openings for ill-judged interventions by the incumbent to the discredit of

Church schools are all too easily created. That there is considerable potential upon which to build is illustrated by a recent survey that showed that the great majority of clergy with Church schools felt very positively about them.[17] Church school governors share with their County school colleagues many challenges and uncertainties. A recent study[18] has highlighted the ambiguities, ambivalences and sometimes bewilderment over their role experienced by many members of governing bodies, whether of Church schools or County. The study shows that the variety of practice suggests at least four 'models' of governing bodies,[19] with a 'woolly' definition of the governors' role frequently being manifested. The closing words of the study are instructive and challenging: '... governing bodies matter. They are more than symbolic. They have a role to perform and this requires a more continuous relationship to their schools than is commonly the case today ... this carries implications for support and training ... it also carries considerable implications for key roles, such as the chairman, headteacher and clerk, and for the style and ethos by which governing bodies function. Service as a school governor is the most common opportunity of public service available to the citizens of their country.'[20] The study notes that the Government Green Paper *Parental Influence at School*[21] asserted the importance of such service and laid out a clearer and more demanding role: 'it remains to be seen whether this is attractive and viable'. Many might think the challenges in these words apply particularly to Church aided schools with their greater autonomous powers and claims to be distinctive, with a special ethos. It might also be thought a very sad thing if, in these times of the Church stressing the practice of stewardship, service as a Church school governor is not perceived to be an attractive and viable form of stewardship.

– And Future

Many of the challenges and opportunities for Church schools in the future have already been touched upon in the selection of certain features from the present scene: the size of schools; the multicultural scenario; the capability to evolve and apply a strategy of provision; more local research; teachers and foundation governors; working out objectives/ethos for

Church schools. They will need to show that they can adapt yet make a distinctive contribution in and to a rapidly changing society. The main speakers at the North of England Conference in 1985 significantly all focused on the theme of change. The first speaker, for example, asked, 'Are we clear about the kind of society we are trying to create? What will be its qualities and values? Is the role to be played by schools and college and adult education and technical training clear?'[22] The speaker asked if we had yet fully grasped the significance of the technological revolution, that 'reckless incursion into the future'. Many changes will be required of schools: new conceptions of achievement; new forms of assessment; new forms of organization; new forms of accountability to mention a few. The second speaker asserted: 'Education in our country is facing, and already undergoing, a radical reconstruction'[23] and ended with a call for 'a new relationship, of partnership and collaborative problem-solving, between leaders in education and leaders in the economic and political spheres and in community life'. The third speaker,[24] with his theme 'The Changing World', provided a challenge for all, not least for the Church, with any continuing involvement in education: 'The world is changing, whether we like it or not (and the British seldom do!) It would be *naive* to pretend it wasn't, *irresponsible* to ignore it, *arrogant* to think you could change it back.'

One thing stands out clearly from these and other writers on the theme of change: any 'partner' wishing to retain an institutional presence in the maintained system of schooling (and higher education), in addition to being able to contribute something distinctive, must also be able to provide the professionalism, expertise, and sophistication required to make an effective contribution to an increasingly demanding educational arena. Seen in this light the recent General Synod motion calling for more resources and a new look for diocesan education committees and education teams is but a very modest reaction. Leslie Paul's comments about the institutional church are relevant: in an increasingly complex education system 'bad or fumbling organisation' is not to be seen 'as an opportunity for the Holy Spirit but simply as waste, lumber, disgrace'.[25] There are already signs that the remaining autonomous powers of voluntary school (and college) governors may be taken over by DES and/or LEAs by stealth if not by a pre-emptive legislative stroke.

It is a familiar observation that life has to be lived with a number of tensions. The alternative to living positively and constructively with tension can be polarisation, fragmentation and disintegration. The changing world will doubtless accentuate many existing tensions and create new ones within which Church schools seek to function. For Church of England schools many of the tensions will cluster around the twin aims of fulfilling a general/community role and a domestic/nurture role, discussed in some depth by the Durham Report[26] and re-iterated during the 1985 General Synod debate.

An increased secularised society and/or an increasingly multifaith society could encourage the tendency to set up private Christian schools (appealing currently mainly to those of a fundamentalist, conservative evangelical persuasion) or to emphasise the 'domestic' or 'nurture' role for aided schools. Speaking to Southwark headteachers in 1985, the Revd Dr Leslie Francis questioned the 'community' or 'service' model and, indeed, the concept of partnership as currently practised, alleging that 'The official response of the Church of England . . . is quick to defend Church schools precisely by denying their distinctiveness.' Dr Francis is currently exploring the suggestion of replacing the 'service' function with a 'prophetic' function, although some who have shared his preliminary thoughts do not see that it necessarily has to be 'either'/'or', but can be 'both'/'and'. In a world of change, with a temptation to want to place one's children in all-Christian schools, in schools that are perhaps of a conservative disposition and thus seen as offering some stability, there can also be a vision of Church schools showing that within the maintained system some schools can creatively hold the tensions that will arise – for example, by offering an educationally respectable religious education without adopting a purely phenomenological approach; by providing in some areas education for children of many faiths where the culture of each can be both honoured and transcended; and by providing the best sort of stability that does not opt out of change. While the country continues to be other than uniform, there will continue to be more than one possible model for Church schools,[27] including scope for more joint or ecumenical schools. The way Church schools present themselves in the future will determine, for example, whether or not Free Church opposition to Church schools, so noticeable forty or so years ago, will continue to decrease as it has done over recent years.[28] Certainly the future could well show that in developing and applying a theology of service there is more potential than Dr Francis seemed inclined to accept, without denying that any Christian institution should also have a prophetic function.

There have recently been within the Church many calls for and reminders of the essential prerequisite of a theological basis for the Church's involvement in education.[29] Theological discourse will both reflect and inform 'the changing world'. Indeed one recent writer on Christian attitudes towards other world religions[30] reminds us of the concept of *kairos*, a special moment in time which is different from ordinary time *(chronos)*. At such a point in history a genuine breakthrough can be made, and the opportunity should not be missed. Are we on the brink of a *kairos* in political, social, economic, educational and theological terms?

The National Society helped to establish and support schools (and training colleges) when an earlier *kairos* was under way. The Church at all levels has to make up its mind if it wants to continue with and provide the necessary means for Church schools as part of its response and contribution to the changing world. At a time when at General Synod and diocesan level the Church is arguing to be taken seriously as a partner in the education service, this essay has tried to give grounds for raising the question of whether the Church is taking and will in the future be seen to be taking itself sufficiently seriously as an important partner.

Different Types of Church School

An *Aided School* is one in which a voluntary body, such as the Church of England, assists in meeting the basic educational needs of an area by providing and maintaining school premises. Central government then gives grant aid to the voluntary body (to the extent of 85 per cent of capital costs, at present rates) and the local education authority shares maintenance costs. The voluntary body has majority representation on the school's governing body and thereby a considerable say in the way the school operates, especially with regard to admissions and the employment of staff.

A *Controlled School* owes its foundation to a voluntary body but under the terms of the 1944 Education Act control has passed to the local authority. The voluntary body has the right to appoint a minority of the governors in order to preserve the school's character in accordance with its trust deed.

In a *Special Agreement School* the staff are employed by the LEA; in other respects Special Agreement Schools are similar to Aided Schools.

1. *What On Earth Is The Church For?*, British Council of Churches and Catholic Truth Society, 1985.
2. J. Murphy, *Church, State and Schools in Britain 1800-1970*, Routledge and Kegan Paul, 1971, page 121.
3. For example:
   The Dual System of County and Voluntary Schools, Socialist Education Association.
   Article by Rick Rodgers in *Where?*, Advisory Centre for Education, No. 179, June 1982, the front cover containing the provocative caption 'Church Schools shall have powers above all others. Time for Reform?'.
   A meeting of the Association of Municipal Authorities, November 1985, carried by one vote a motion calling for a fundamental change in the 'dual system'. Reported in *Education* 15th November 1985, page 452.
4. For example, in *Better Schools*, Department of Education and Science and Welsh Office, HMSO, 1985.
5. *Op. cit.*, page 129.
6. See DES statistics.
7. John D. Gay, *The Size of Anglican Primary Schools*, Culham College Institute Occasional Paper No. 7, 1985.
8. *Ibid.*, page 4.
9. H.A. Williams, *Some Day I'll Find You*, Mitchell Beazley, 1982, page 103.
10. *Schools and Multicultural Education*, General Synod Board of Education Discussion Paper 1/84.
11. David Clark, *Can the Church in Education Save its Soul? Crosscurrent No. 17*, National Society, July 1985.
12. *Crosscurrent No. 18*, National Society, October 1985, page 10.
13. *Education for All*, Report of the Committee of Inquiry into the Education of Children from Ethnic Minority Groups, HMSO, 1985.
14. Alan Brown, *Church and School*, a personal reflection upon the present state of Religious Education in Church of England Aided Schools, (unpublished).
15. *A Future in Partnership*, National Society, 1984, page 69.
16. Leslie J. Francis, *Partnership in Rural Education*, Collins, 1986.
17. *Gallup Survey of Church of England Clergymen*, prepared for the Archbishop's Commission on Urban Priority Areas, General Synod of the Church of England, 1986, page 18.

18. Maurice Kogan (Editor), *School Governing Bodies,* Heinemann Educational Books, 1984.
19. *Ibid.,* chapter 8.
20. *Ibid.,* page 180.
21. *Parental Influence at School,* DES and Welsh Office, HMSO, 1984.
22. Professor John Tomlinson CBE, *Crossing the Bridge;* Presidential Address at the North of England Education Conference, Huddersfield, 1986.
23. Professor Ian Lister, *Reconstructing Teacher Education,* address at the North of England Education Conference.
24. Professor Charles Handy, *The Changing World,* address at the North of England Education Conference.
25. Leslie Paul, *The Death and Resurrection of the Church,* Hodder and Stoughton, 1968, page 75.
26. *The Fourth R,* The Durham Report on R.E., National Society and S.P.C.K., 1970.
27. See *A Future in Partnership,* pages 99-102.
28. *Church Schools,* A Discussion Document, Free Church Federal Council Education Committee, 1984.
29. See, for example, *The Fourth R,* chapter 2, *A Future in Partnership,* chapter 4, and the Archbishop of Canterbury's and the Bishop of London's speeches in the 1985 General Synod debate, reproduced in *Positive Partnership,* National Society, 1985.
30. Paul F. Knitter, *No Other Name?,* Maryknoll Orbis, 1985, page 18.

8

A Church Primary School in a Multicultural Setting

David Barton

Any mention of Soho brings to mind a kind of adult education not usually associated with the National Society, so perhaps it is necessary to set the scene for a multicultural primary school in a red light area, only two minutes from the snarled-up traffic of Piccadilly Circus.

In most respects the basic picture is typical of many other multicultural schools: Victorian buildings, the product of philanthropy and the days of Christian confidence, now in the middle of a patchily deprived community, and set in a parish where the numerical decline in membership is at its lowest level. In the early seventies the problems faced by the school were those faced by a number of others. A sudden wave of immigration, in this case from Hong Kong, had built up a largely non-English-speaking child and parent population. By 1975 this was 65 per cent Cantonese speaking, the remaining children being roughly equal groups of Bengali, Spanish and Italian speakers. There were only two English-speaking children in the whole school, and none who claimed Anglican allegiance. The governing body, drawn from a grand church on the other side of Piccadilly Circus, was white, kindly, middle-aged to elderly, and wholly bewildered by its role in such a setting. The teachers on the staff, all but one monolingual English speakers, were almost entirely without strategies to deal with the children who sat in front of them day by day.

In many ways Soho should have been able to manage

such a situation. In the seventeenth century it was built as a north London suburb and has been populated by successive waves of immigration – Swiss, Italian, Spanish, Jews from Germany and from Eastern Europe and, in recent years Chinese from Hong Kong and Bengalis from Bangladesh. The original Parish School was founded in 1699 by the churchwardens of St Anne's. Their resources were slender and there were many doubts about whether the school could keep going. But, faced with large numbers of children on the streets falling into crime and other moral danger, they pressed on, believing that it was right to do so because of the importance of the endeavour. Their determined and enlightened struggle (at a very early stage they began, unusually, to provide education for girls) gives both a spur and a comforting sense of continuity to the present-day school. When immigration from Hong Kong stopped abruptly in 1979 and caused a rapid decline in the roll, with closure a possibility, for anyone who had read the records it was a familiar tale, as was the anxiety about finding the money to patch up our leaking roof. We have, not for the first time, survived. The school is again full, and even the roof is sound. There are even good grounds for believing that the tidal wave of vice that washed right up to the school gates with its shops, cinemas and peep-shows is receding in the face of more effective legislation. The record of that is for other literature.

This essay is an attempt to catalogue the developments in the school over the past ten years, and in doing so to examine some of the questions raised by the involvement of a Church primary school in a multicultural, multifaith setting. It seems simpler to divide this into three, essentially coherent, parts: the curriculum, relationships with parents and the wider community, and the place of religious education in a school where other historic faiths are in a majority.

From the beginning the most important task has been to ensure that the curriculum, whether in respect of individuals or the whole class, does not founder on 'the language problem'. The fact that we have in our classes large numbers of non-English-speaking children (and at times that has been over 80 per cent of the roll) has been a source of justifiable anxiety to all of us. Yet all our experience suggests that, despite every pressure to do so, it is very important not to concentrate too narrowly on the issue of teaching English as a second language. The inevitable result of that is a narrowing of the curriculum and a slowing down of learning. Paradoxically, by valuing children's home languages and the culture implied by them, and by maintaining as broad a curriculum as possible, not only can we keep the process of learning moving forward, but the development of English language becomes easier and more natural. For the past two years we have been able to teach Bengali children in their mother tongue for one day a week. During the same period their spoken and written English has made far more rapid progress than in the period before.

Conversely, if children have felt that their home language is devalued by the attitude of the school (all too easy when teachers are anxious about progress), not simply their English but the whole range of their achievement is impaired. By using art, music, dance and movement we have provided a wide range of communication between teacher and child. In practice the processes involved in these areas provide a stimulus for language and a sense of achievement that both motivates and rewards. It is here that the cultural background of children can best be expressed, through art or music, through an investigation of the different number systems, through a comparison of different orthographies, or sharing the stories for each cultural tradition. In the hands of a gifted teacher (and in this respect the school has been very fortunate) who has been able to bring these experiences into a coherent whole, the curriculum has gained a quite extraordinary power and momentum. Children have become deeply engaged, their imaginations absorbed, and clearly new ways of thinking and working have been established that would influence each child long after they have left us. Just as important, the standards achieved have been comparable with any school in more favoured circumstances.

Detailed curriculum-planning around these basic aims is fundamental to everything we do. And nowhere is this relationship between planned, organised learning founded on children's own experiences and the long-term influence we should have as teachers more important than in the area of relationships between different nationalities, both within the school and outside it. Racism is always a factor, for the most part outlawed but never curbed by our disapproval. As we have allowed the cultural setting of the school to be our agenda and helped children to see some of the depths and sophistication of each other's backgrounds, the abuse and tension have diminished visibly. If racism is at least in part about stereotyping, then a curriculum that can show the complexity of individuals and their culture becomes a powerful tool to combat it.

At an early stage of our planning, when we were in considerable need of resources and support, we turned to the parents for help. A key appointment had been that of a home-school worker, herself Cantonese-speaking. Through her we found links with a community that was otherwise closed to us, and in consequence we were offered a greater source of curriculum support than any LEA could offer. Encouraged by her, parents came into our classes and, through translators, explained details of Chinese and Bengali customs, telling stories of their childhood, involving children in cooking and in calligraphy. Our whole policy of mother-tongue support has largely depended on the help that they have given. When this began we were too involved in the sheer excitement of the process to weigh its significance. It was only later that we realised that we have taken the unusual step of involving parents centrally in the curriculum of the school. Doing this in our particular context, we had made it possible for the parents to grasp and evaluate a form of teaching that was totally different from their own educational experiences. We pay too little heed, as teachers, to the problems faced by families in sending their children to our schools, and this underestimation of the vulnerability of parents is doubly so when we do not communicate in a common language. We have begun to realise how difficult it is for many to see their children growing away from their own traditional values and culture, learning to speak English and adapting to our society so much more easily than any adult can. The parents' partnership with us and our obvious need of their skills have made it possible for them to gain confidence in themselves in a situation that might otherwise have been devaluing and alienating.

This insight highlighted the need for the school to be more widely involved in the surrounding community. We had, as a separate development, offered the use of our limited space to the local community. Residents' associations, a Kung

Fu Club and a Chinese mother-tongue school have become regular users, and this has helped to link us to a local community from which we had become isolated by language and culture. But there were some specific needs that clearly merited special attention. One was for more sensitivity and care in the running of language courses for adults. Many women, in particular, opted out of formally structured classes, because nothing in their cultural background gave them an image of themselves as learners. The most pressing need that emerged was that of under-fives' care and support. Census returns for the area are unreliable; because no needs were recorded, no services are provided. With only one childminder in the area, there was, a few years ago, a distressing amount of evidence of poor childminding arrangements.

The Governors decided that a first call on our spare space should be for a day nursery. The school itself has had its own nursery for many years. After discussions with the LEA, Social Services and voluntary agency working in this field, a day nursery was set up to cater for children of eighteen months and upwards. The Diocesan Board funded the necessary alterations to the building, and the whole project took less than a year – a good example of the flexibility of the voluntary aided system. Comparable local authority projects have measured the time in years.

This range of developments has had considerable effect on the way in which the school sees itself and on the way it works. *Faith in the City*[1] rightly emphasises the importance of the community school. Our experience would suggest the need to place the emphasis (at least in the primary school) less on community and more on family support. The degree of stress in the inner city is marked, and families clearly go through a number of difficulties at different stages of children's growth. The school is often the place where the warning bells are sounded, but all too often we are ill equipped to help. The changed pattern of the school's life has made us, as a staff, look again at our own role. Over the past three years we have had regular in-service discussions with a psychotherapist so that our response to distressed children and their families becomes more skilled and effective. Seeing ourselves with a dual role, educators (the priority) and agents of family support (even if that often simply means listening and then making a referral to the appropriate agency) seems to be the right role for the Church school in our setting.

There had been a long tradition in the school of the curate visiting each week to instruct the ten- and eleven-year-old children in the Book of Common Prayer, regardless of the faith or language of the child. The problem was less one of how to replace this with something else, more of how we could reconcile our status as a Church school with the fact that the majority of our families were from other world faiths than Christianity. If one adds to that an awareness that for all our families, of any faith or none, we are the only maintained school in the area, this becomes the most sensitive issue we have to face. As a primary school teacher, I have always felt that discussions of this issue are too often blurred by perspectives and preoccupations of a purely adult kind. It is too easily forgotten that at this early developmental stage, while children can grasp differences, they are much more concerned with the spiritual elements of religion than with the theological. We have also attempted to be as aware as we can of the inner world of children, of the ways in which they come to terms with the growing and changing elements in their lives, of friendship and loss, happiness, loneliness, fear, anger, awe. Through these children develop their own individual ways of looking at life, and it is in these areas that the world's great faiths always speak. The value and meaning of religion to any child ultimately depends on his or her ability to impinge on this inner shaping. There are clearly objective elements in Christianity and other faiths that we should teach. But we have also tried to discover how to use the stories and celebrations of both Christianity and other faiths in a way that lays the foundations for the faith of a mature adult, and in a way that enables children to see that Christianity, as much as Islam, Hinduism or Buddhism, opens up a way of thinking and feeling and looking at life that is both meaningful and rewarding.

As I have taken children on pilgrimages to the various temples, churches and ashrams that are dotted about Central London, I have become aware of our need to develop a proper attitude of humility; partly that is because we have sponsored so much bad RE, but mostly because we are, in schools like my own, in an almost uncharted area of exploration.

I can only say that my own encounters with other faiths

over the past years have served to enrich my understanding of Christianity and enlarged my perception of the spiritual life. There is much here from which we could all learn. I have space for two significant shifts in the way we have worked. One is the discovery of the importance of narrative story-telling, long lost in Western Christianity but still present in the traditions I discovered in my setting. A very large part of what we want to say can be conveyed in the story, especially when the teller has so absorbed the narrative that the children lose themselves in it and instinctively appreciate the elements that link with their own inner meaning. The wealth of stories that cluster round the historic faiths of the world is extraordinary. And of course, such a discovery brings us back full circle to the foundation documents of our own Bible. Storytelling is an art the Church could do well to revive. The second, and unexpected discovery (in a school context) was that of the experience of meditation, prayer and above all of commonly held silence – a wholly central element in all world faiths. On a recent visit to our local Hindu ashram, I was yet again struck by the way in which the children had an instinctive feel for the importance of the tasks of praying going on around them. They walked around carefully, avoiding the paths of devotees as they crossed and recrossed the floor, clearly aware that they were privileged to be there. As a school we make a similar search. One assembly each week is devoted to the exploration of silence, to physical ways of holding ourselves in quiet, and the privacy of an inner personal world. To explore religious education in this way is not, I hope, to fail the expectations of the Church. I hope, too, that it is acceptable to the simple devout families of other faiths who are such a large proportion of our parents, and whose influence on their children contributes so much to the positive atmosphere and purpose of the school.

The issue of religious education highlights a difficulty that affects all aspects of work in a Church school, namely, the unspoken pressures from both the Church and those outside it about the tasks we have as teachers. Because Christianity and Christian education have contributed so much to British culture, there is a general assumption that in this, as in other ways, in a changing world the Church will stand for unchanging values. This expectation needs to be carefully weighed, for it can be an unjustified brake on proper development. It was certainly hard for us to reach the point where cultural and religious diversity were seen to be an asset, and even harder to move on to use that diversity in the implementation of the curriculum. There is an imaginative leap to be taken, not normally asked of English Christians, to see Christianity as a world faith, itself culturally diverse, whose founder was brownish, not white, and which in the developing world at least needs to win its place in the structure of a society by the effectiveness of its performance. To a large extent this is the situation of most inner-city schools, where the assumption by many LEA officers is that a Church school is an inappropriate agent for multicultural education. One of the disappointments of *Faith in the City* is that it failed to see that in an encounter with a changing, emergent society, it is the Church school that is often in the front line rather than the parish church. All too frequently the Christian faith is judged itself for good or ill by what we do. This clearly points to the need for more awareness in dioceses of the significance of their multiracial schools. Imaginative planning by governing bodies and effective resourcing by diocesan boards may also be called for. The fact that so many multiracial schools are in a deprived setting suggests a need for more links with Boards for Social Responsibility and the possible funding of support workers. Above all, there is the need for the pooling of experiences in order to evaluate them and see ways forward, and not just for our own sake. Precisely because we are placed in the middle of the changing point of our society, schools like my own (of which there are now surely many) may have skills and insights for the Church as a whole. A multiracial, multifaith society may soon have as much significance for a rural village as it does for Soho's Urban Village.

1. *Faith in the City:* A Call for Action by Church and Nation, The Report of the Archbishop of Canterbury's Commission on Urban Priority Areas, Church House Publishing, 1985.

9

The Anglican Colleges of Higher Education

Clive Jones-Davies

Early nineteenth-century initiatives in education included not only the establishment of schools under the aegis of the British and Foreign Schools Society and of the National Society, but arrangements by both Societies for the training of teachers. As schools proliferated throughout England and Wales, the need to establish a trained professional body of teachers also increased and, as with schools, it was the Church and not the State which responded to this task. By the end of the first half of the century many Anglican Colleges had been established to which were added, from the middle of the century onwards, Roman Catholic, Congregational and Methodist Colleges. Not until the early years of the twentieth century were the first Local Education Authority colleges established. By 1969 local authority involvement had over-taken that of the Churches but about one-third of the system still reflected the Church's original witness in this important area, there being 107 local education authority colleges of education and 51 voluntary colleges. Of these, 27 were of Anglican foundation. Rationalisation of the teacher training system in the 1970s has reduced the Churches' involvement to seventeen institutions, four of which are larger, mixed economy or federated organisations within which previously independent Church colleges play a significant role. Another College, Homerton, Cambridge, survives as a non-denominational voluntary college having been established in 1852 by the Congregationalists.

In continuing to involve itself in education by the support of such colleges, the Anglican Church lays itself open to the charge of misinterpreting its mission and misdirecting its witness in relation to the needs of modern society. The charge may be extended to include the Church's role in primary and secondary school provision and the Roman Catholic and Methodist Churches also stand accused. Church men and women, as well as those outside the Churches may be counted with the accusers. Certainly the state has now largely taken over the responsibilities which the Churches fulfilled, particularly in the maintenance of educational establishments. The sense of responsibility which brought about the inversion of the respective contributions of Church and State was linked to the State's increased capacity to fund initiatives from central and local taxation. However, although Church influence was thereby weakened, it remains sufficiently strong to affect the character of the overall system and to make a vital contribution to that system.

The Church's resolve to maintain an institutional presence in education is often taken for protectionism, a demand for its historic rights. This is to ignore the concept of education held by responsible Christians, namely that there is a distinctive Christian view of the content and practice of education involving specific perceptions of the curriculum and of styles of engagement in the learning process. The argument that the Church should now withdraw from its commitment is also unconvincing because, as in many other spheres of social service, a partnership has been developed which demands a particular contribution by the Church to complement that made by the state. In education the new role is more akin to that exercised in child care than in the health service, in the maintenance of children's homes than of hospitals, but, in all these spheres, Church and state coexist to serve.

The particular role to be played by the Church is one which can more properly and successfully be fulfilled by having responsibility *for* institutions, both colleges and schools, rather than limited responsibility *in* institutions. The nature of the exercise demands this. Stephen Prickett *In Praise of Institutions* in Michael Pye's *The Language of the Church in Higher and Further Education* (1977) states that 'the important quality of institutions is not their permanence but their capacity for change. We must follow T.S. Eliot in defining "tradition" not as repetition, but as innovation.[1] This change and innovation involves institutional and personal metamorphosis. Church colleges have responded to changing needs and have developed as institutions: they grew in size with the demand for more teachers, they became co-educational in response to the increase in the number of women students and they were the first colleges outside the universities to offer BA and BSc degrees. It is the capacity of the institutions to change the individual which is the more important factor, however. Religion and education are both committed to influencing the individual through change towards maturity and fulfilment and this affinity of aim is basic to the justification of the Church's involvement in education. Change in itself is justified only in terms of the improvement to which it leads. In the processes which change the individual, whether at school or in higher education, the Church has an interest. It is itself a medium for change and within its ministry should be counted those who serve in schools, colleges and universities.

Despite the controversies which have raged in some European countries about the role of the Church in education, this shared concern for the individual human being has been one of the most attractive characteristics of our civilisation. Even when the churches have relinquished their primacy in education, this major aim of helping each individual to develop and become truly fulfilled has, so far, been retained. However, there is a danger that if the influence of the Church is lost, this aim may be diluted.

Where the Anglican Church has maintained its institutional role it can influence and direct the processes of change, but where its influence is more diffuse and dependent on the vitality of the leaven as represented by isolated individuals or groups of individuals it is less efficient in directing change. That specifically Christian emphasis within the system is weakened. It is true that individuals or groups of individuals within institutions are in varying degrees able to affect institutions, as is witnessed by the role of chaplains in our colleges, polytechnics and universities. Such influence, however, is limited by the scale of the task and suffers further from a lack of continuity when individuals vacate posts. Even where there is a statutory foundation for the work of the

Church within an institution, as in the case of religious educa-tion in County schools, its impact is variable and considerably less effective than that achieved in voluntary schools.

If the image of leaven in bread has validity in the context of education it is when it is extended to refer to Church schools and colleges, these being regarded as the leaven within the total system. This is how the contribution of the Church is best made. Abolition of the voluntary sector or closure of more Church colleges, of whatever denomination, would remove or reduce to an ineffectual level that Christian influence which has characterised the system hitherto. What was initially a Christian, religiously inspired venture would become a chiefly humanistic, secular undertaking. The opportunity for the expression of a distinctively Christian view would be lost.

It is interesting to consider whether if the State had not become the chief provider of education, the Church would have developed a different model of colleges than it supports at present. Given that somehow funding would have become available, either by direct endowment or by the state paying the piper but not calling the tune, namely by making the Church its agent, it is almost inevitable that large institutions would have developed for the same reasons of scale economies which have dictated the pattern of our present system. Nevertheless, it is conceivable that, by a conscious decision to ensure that emphasis on community which characterises our present Church colleges, large institutions would have been organised in such a way as to mitigate the effect of their impersonality or a diverse system of large and small institutions would have been established. In a more constructive, stable climate for development, conscious decisions based on the balance of advantage between large institutions where the priority is the unit of cost and smaller, acceptably costed, provisions, with greater emphasis on a personal supportive dimension, would have been possible. A conscious decision to create and maintain smaller, collegiate style institutions is likely to have been made because of the perceived worth of such establishments.

Church colleges are as a group much smaller than other establishments of higher education, the largest college having just over 1600 students and the more usual size being of the order of 1000. They are much more akin to the old-style monotechnic Colleges of Education, from which all of them have developed. With one exception, however, they have embraced a policy of diversification and now offer a range of B.A and B.Sc. provision. This diversification has been determined by the compatibility of the new courses offered with the colleges' continuing emphasis on teacher training. Because of their comparatively autonomous self-governing nature they have been able to respond quickly to national needs and continue to do so, as is seen in the development of new courses such as those applicable to nursing and paramedical professions. Such courses fall within the genre of personal service courses where the teaching refers to training for specific tasks related to the care or development of the individual or a service to the community. In such courses, Christian or, if not specifically expressed as such, religious values are operative.

This type of course, where the student is prepared for a career involving service or ministry to others is well provided for within a college which lays emphasis on community living, and where students find an opportunity for development of their individual and social being in a context where social interaction is never far away from expressed Christian concepts, and where the institution's own policy for corporate life is based on such concepts. The personal identity of a student comes to be realised in terms of his relationships where each perceives the other in terms of dimensions of personal worth and social value. Doubtless larger communities with a richer variety of academic courses also have social opportunities within which the individual will develop. However, the ambience of such institutions is less easy to perceive in terms of totality. Church colleges offer social as well as academic opportunities and those social opportunities are founded on principles, explicit as well as implicit, to do with the quality of relationships between individuals and between the individual and God. For this to be effectively perceived, formal and obvious manifestations of the Christian life need to be present: the chapel and the chaplaincy, regular services and the celebration of Christian festivals, and a close relationship between the College and parishes and church schools are such manifestations.

The task of the Church college is not perceived to be the provision of the same under another name, 'voluntary', but the creation of a genuine choice of institutions for students. A choice is provided, at the broadest level, between generally smaller and predominantly residential colleges emphasising a Christianity-based community, and larger more freely structured institutions where the emphasis is less obviously upon a collegiate common life. There is undeniably a difference between such institutional organisations and the experiences of those attending significantly differ. It would be arrogant and untrue for Church colleges to claim to have a monopoly of those experiences which create the best professionals, or to be the only communities which are capable of producing responsible, committed or compassionate practitioners. What they may claim is that they seek to demonstrate, in their perception of tasks and in the way they carry them out, particular values which are themselves extra to, or stand instead of, values which underlie the work of more secular institutions. Many students consciously seek such colleges because of this specific religious emphasis, others because of their size and of their tradition of close community life. The students themselves contribute to the ethos of the colleges because of their particular motivation. Certainly, the recruitment record of our colleges testifies to their popularity and their record of job acquisition by students testifies to their success.

Because of their distinctiveness and to distinguish more properly the role to be played by the Church colleges, the title 'voluntary', which is in any event of dubious validity in the strict sense of self-sufficiency of funding, should be replaced by the title 'Christian'. This would clarify the Church's position in relation to other providers and would focus attention on a specific role to be played by such colleges which is not merely a replication of the role of other non-Church-linked institutions. This would comply also with the government's view of a diversified higher education system as described in the Green Paper *The Development of Higher Education into the 1990s*. 'The Government has no wish to impose a uniform pattern on higher education; on the contrary the Government would like to see even greater vitality and flexibility'.[2]

Current developments in terms of greater collaboration between the Anglican colleges, involving joint initiatives in the provision of courses and the sharing of staff and resources, will further strengthen the group as a whole and each college individually. Such confederation will come to be recognised as a specific, well defined section extended, it is hoped, to include Roman Catholic and Methodist colleges within the total higher education system in England and Wales. This will take further the planning collaboration made possible by the Voluntary Sector Consultative Council which relates the voluntary colleges' initiatives to those of the remainder of the public sector within the National Advisory Body.

This co-ordinated, effective involvement will ensure that the present-day colleges keep faith with those who from the early days of the nineteenth century have maintained for the Church the opportunity of making within higher education its own distinctive contribution.

1. *The Language of the Church in Higher and Further Education,* edited by Michael Pye, The Bradwell Consultation, 1977, page 15.
2. *The Development of Higher Education into the 1990s,* HMSO, 1985.

Epilogue:
The National Society into the Future

Colin Alves

From one point of view it is a measure of real success that so many people nowadays need to ask 'What is the National Society?' The joint operation between the Society and the General Synod Board of Education which has been in existence now for twelve years was intended not only to remove unnecessary duplication of effort but also to ensure that the Church of England was not inadvertently speaking with a dangerously divided voice on matters educational. It must therefore be counted as a form of 'success' that many people now believe the Board of Education to be the only central body in the Church of England operating in the field of education. Another measure of this 'success' is to be found in the fact that *A Future in Partnership* (published by the NS) was followed so rapidly by a General Synod debate in which the central concerns of the Society's document were incorporated into a Synod policy statement.

Looking back over these past twelve years many people are apt to forget (if they ever knew!) that the 1972 agreement between the Board and the Society (which led to the appointment of a joint General Secretary in 1974) was not the first attempt to link the work of the Society with the central structures of the Church. Almost forty years earlier (as the Dean of Chichester reminds us in his essay) the Society had been recognised as the Church's Central Council for Religious Education, and it was the *Society's* officers who 'did much of the spade-work on the religious clauses' of the 1944 Act on behalf of the Church. Even after the Church Assembly in

1947 set up its own Council for Education (replaced by the Board of Education in 1958), the Society continued to be regarded as a significant voice speaking on behalf of the Church of England. Certainly as late at 1979 the Department of Education and Science was sending parallel copies of its consultative letters both to the Board and to the Society. It was only during the early 1980s that the practice arose of sending all such correspondence solely to the Board.

DES officials had known, of course, from 1974 onwards that no matter to which of the two addresses they sent such a letter the same person would answer it. But it gradually became apparent, to *all* parties concerned, that an authoritative reply 'on behalf of the Church of England' had to be routed through the synodical structures rather than through the associated voluntary body.

It is in this context, therefore, that the question of the future role of the National Society has to be answered. Assuming (as we must, at least for the time being) that the General Synod Board of Education continues to exist, with roughly the present terms of reference, what should the Society be doing, other than give general 'support' to the work of the Board by contributing to the salaries of the jointly appointed staff?

One perhaps rather negative way of coming at the same question is to ask a) what the Board would find itself unable to do if the Society's financial support were withdrawn and b) what the Board is in any case unable to do because of its constitutional position. Answers to these two questions should provide some indication of where the National Society's continuing role should lie. Perhaps the negative form of the question prompts (or presupposes) a negative form of the answer, namely that the Society should not move into areas of work, new for it, which the Board is well equipped to service already. Even though the Society's Chárter rightly gives it the power to operate over a wide field, practical considerations would make it unwise for the Society to exercise that power to the full at the present time. It should not, for example, seek to operate directly in the world of the Sunday school, or of the Youth Club, or even of Adult Education. The Society should (at least for the foreseeable future) continue to focus its work where it always has been focused, namely in its concern that the general education of the nation at large shall be founded upon Christian principles.

The General Synod, through the Board of Education, as has already been stressed, shares that commitment and has indeed as recently as July 1985 reaffirmed its 'concern for the well-being of the whole of the maintained system of education in this country and its expectation that it will continue to play a significant role as a national partner within that system'.[1] But the Board as currently funded, *without* the support of the Society, would be quite unable to deal with the bulk of requests for advice and information about the workings of the maintained system which flood into Church House each week both from the dioceses and from individual schools.

The requests fall mainly into two categories – those to do with legal and financial matters, and those to do with the curriculum of schools, particularly in relation to religious education. For the former, the Society's officers are able to call upon the advice and support of Lee, Bolton and Lee (currently in the person of Mr Peter Beesley), and it is fervently to be hoped that the Society will be able to go on providing the quality of service in this area which the present arrangements allow. The legal service supplied by Lee, Bolton and Lee is supported and supplemented, of course, by the availability of the Society's archives, and here again it will be important for the Society to maintain this particular operation – and indeed develop it.

In the second area – the school curriculum – the Society looks to its RE Resource Centres for the provision of advice, and increasingly the advice sought is to do with the curriculum in general (including the hidden curriculum), not just with RE as a 'subject'. This is to be welcomed. It is not that 'RE as a subject' is unimportant – far from it; it is becoming more crucial and critical every day – but providing 'education' founded upon Christian principles' is not *just* a matter of ensuring that RE is somewhere on the timetable (though it *is* that as well).

It is in this area that perhaps the future role of the Society will most firmly lie. As we have indicated, the Board of Education is never likely to be sufficiently funded to provide the advisory services available through the Society, but even if it were it would still find major difficulties in tackling the issues surrounding the school curriculum. Being a body within a synodical structure it is subject to synodical constraints. It is accountable to Synod for its every pronouncement, however guarded, exploratory and tentative that pronouncement may be. In contrast, the National Society is entirely its own master. The very characteristic which has made the Society inappropriate as a consultative body for the DES makes it highly appropriate as a body which can itself open issues, initiate discussions, challenge current assumptions.

This role is of course not unfamiliar to the Society. The commissioning and publication of the *Durham Report* on Religious Education (1970) was entirely a National Society initiative. So was the commissioning and publication of the *Carlisle Report* on the role of the diocese in education (1971), and of its 'sequel', the report on *Sector Ministries* (1983). Fresh in everyone's memory is of course the publication of *A Future in Partnership* (1984) which, as was noted above, led directly to the setting up of a General Synod debate. This last example illustrates very well not only the close working of the Society and the Board of Education but also their complementary natures. *A Future in Partnership* flew a large number of kites (and trailed an equal number of coats) which would never have found their way into a report whose purpose was to form a policy statement for endorsement by Synod. But the kites were worth flying – many of them are still up in the air and some may even yet find their way (in a modified form, perhaps) into Synodical documents of the future.

But this structural, constitutional independence is not the only advantage the Society has. It has an important financial independence, which enables flexibility of action. Synod-related budgets have to be drawn up virtually twelve to eighteen months in advance of anticipated expenditure. There is little room there for the rapid establishment of any unplanned working party to tackle some issue which has suddenly become important to the Church. But the Society does have the power to do just that.

The power derives, of course, from the fact that the Society's funding comes not from any mechanically calculated quota, but from the investments of past members and the subscriptions and donations of present ones. And this has the further advantage that there is, potentially at least, a sense amongst the members of being closely involved in the concerns and activities of the Society as a whole. This involvement is no monochrome affair. The membership of the Society will almost inevitably continue to include those working in schools, in colleges, in diocesan offices, in parishes – teachers, administrators, governors, theologians – from a wide variety of urban and rural situations, throughout the whole of England and Wales (the latter providing the special insights which come a) from operating in education as a disestablished Church and b) from the challenges and complexities of bilingual education).

The future of the Society, as I see it, will be shaped by its two main strengths – flexibility of action and wide member involvement. Working from this dual base the Society should continue to maintain (and, where appropriate, develop) its direct advisory services, but should also give increasing attention to its programme of publications. It should build on the excellent pioneering work of the *Crosscurrent* venture. It should also commission longer manuscripts for publication, exploring in particular the new political issues which are beginning to confront us (the use of 'vouchers', the introduction of 'Crown schools', the future of the independent sector) as well as the curricular issues raised by Professor Mitchell and Dr Hargreaves (amongst others) in this present volume. Indeed this present volume is itself a good example of the sort of thing which needs to be, and so clearly can be, achieved by the Society.

The Society will also continue to provide the administrative service it offers in relation to various Trusts, as well as being the national focus for projects such as the Urban Studies Centre Consortium and the Church Colleges' Religious Studies Certificate programme. Perhaps it will, by the end of the century, have found the opportunity at last to fulfil the fifth aim of its 1953 policy statement, the establishment of a 'register of Church teachers'. Such a move would certainly meet one of the concerns expressed in the General Synod debate of July 1985 (Motion 15 (c)),[2] but the difficulties involved should not be underestimated. (It has been difficult enough to compile just a register of Church schools!) But such a suggestion raises the deeper issue of the extent to which the Society (drawing upon the resources available through the very width of its membership) should accept a pastoral as well as an administrative and an advisory role in relation to those engaged in the work of the schools.

That may well be an important development in the years ahead. What will always remain crucial, however, is that the Society retains its role as a motivator and enabler of *action* which implements its basic purpose – that the educational system of England and Wales shall continue to be imbued with the insights and concerns of the Christian gospel. Whatever else may or may not change, *that* must remain constant.

1. *Positive Partnership,* National Society, 1985, page 50.
2. *Ibid.*

Index

Index

Temple, William, Archbishop of Canterbury   27, 28, 33
Thatcher, Margaret   30
Thorne, BL   31
Todhunter, JLB   29
Tomlinson, John   78
Trinity College, Carmarthen   22

Urban Studies Centre Consortium   99

Voluntary Sector Consultative Council   93

Waddington, Robert   62, 64, 65
Watson, Joshua   19, 23, 25
Webster, AB   25
Wedderspoon, AG   25
Whitelands College   21
Willey, Basil   49, 52
Williams, HA   69, 77
Wilson, Harold   53

York Minster   40
York RE Centre   33

107

Acknowledgements

The National Society thanks the following for permission to quote from the named publications:

George Allen and Unwin Ltd: *Gifford Lectures,* H H Price, 1969

A and C Black Ltd: *The Victorian Church,* Owen Chadwick, 1970

The Bradwell Consultation: *The Language of the Church in Higher and Further Education,* Michael Pye (editor), 1977

Chatto and Windus: *Seventeenth Century Background,* Basil Willey, 1934

Chelmsford Diocesan Council for Education and Training: *A Task for all Christians,* 1982

Collins Liturgical Publications: The Bishop of London's Preface to *Partnership in Rural Education,* Leslie J Francis, 1986

The Controller of Her Majesty's Stationery Office: *The Development of Higher and Further Education into the 1990s,* 1985

Culham College Institute: *The Size of Anglican Primary Schools,* John D Gay, 1985

Heinemann Educational Books: *School Governing Bodies,* Maurice Kogan (editor), 1984

Hodder and Stoughton Ltd: *The Death and Resurrection of the Church,* Leslie Paul, 1968

The Hockerill Educational Foundation: *The Unknown, Remembered Gate,* a lecture by Robert Waddington, 1985

Macmillan Publishers Ltd: *Church and State in English Education,* M Cruickshank, 1963 and *The Church Looks Forward,* 1984

Routledge and Kegan Paul Ltd: *Church, State and Schools in Britain 1800-1970,* J Murphy, 1971 and *The Sovereignty of Good,* Iris Murdoch, 1970

Times Newspapers Ltd: *The Times,* 29th May 1839

What Others Say
About #yourmoney

"#yourmoney will help you take control of your finances, guide you in making some of the most important financial decisions of your life and help you understand the basics of banking so it works for rather than against you. It is an accessible read and one that you can keep referring to over time."
– Lily LaPenna, founder and CEO of MyBnk

***

"Today's students are entering a world of record tuition fees and rising unemployment and a slew of money management books have hit the shelves in response. Jeannette A Lichner's *#yourmoney* takes a pared-down approach to some of the most tedious but inevitable financial issues facing young people today. The result is a veritable survival guide to the scary world of finance: from HMRC, to student loans, to achievable savings goals.

There are a few very basic money-saving tips, such as 'avoid getting mugged', but the accessible language, personal anecdotes and inspirational quotes make it one of the more manageable additions to the financial books marketplace.

For veterans of the financial crisis, and financially astute young adults, there will be no huge revelations here. But for young people setting out on the road to financial independence, *#yourmoney* will be a must-read."
– Regional newspaper book review

***

"This is a personal finance book for real people in the real world – two hundred and thirty pages jammed full of common sense, wisdom, and practical information that everyone needs to know."
– Isaac T Tabner CFA, DipPfs, personal finance lecturer

***

"I found #yourmoney to be bite-size, relevant and engaging. Though aimed at the 16–25 age bracket, I think its teachings are very worthwhile for people of older ages too. Nice work!"
– James, 28

***

"As with many educational books, a great many would rather simply Google for what they need to know. In this case, I would strongly advise otherwise. The advice and information I gained from reading *#yourmoney* was invaluable. The clarity and detail which Jeanette provides help in explaining how important it is to be on top of one's personal finances. In the same way a tourist might take a Lonely Planet abroad, I think everyone should take this book with them through senior school, university, and the start of a career."
– Piers, graduate student starting his first job

***

"Everyone buy this book about money!! It is very interesting and something you will definitely use throughout the years. You all know I only endorse things that I believe in."
– Kadeza, senior school student, via Facebook

***

"We will recommend this book to the sixth form for extra reading because it is an excellent resource, very useful and clearly set out."
– Senior school headmistress

***

"This excellent and much-needed book fills a gap for parents and for their offspring, and for once the publisher's blurb and the strap line are WYSIWYG: it really does answer all the important questions about earning, spending and saving for the teenager, for the university student, and for others. Jeannette Lichner puts across her lessons in a clear prose style, which commands attention without – as it could easily be – being bossy, and there is a bright idea, clever note or vital tip on nearly every page. *#yourmoney* kept my undergraduate daughter absorbed in the back of the car, and once she had